BRIGHT WINGS
DAPPLED THINGS

MISIT ANGELV
M
S
VVM

BRIGHT WINGS
DAPPLED THINGS

The Poems of

GERARD MANLEY HOPKINS SJ

With Photographs by

FR FRANCIS BROWNE SJ

Introduction and Commentary

JO O'DONOVAN RSM

Published by Messenger Publications, 2018

Extract from 'Hopkins in Kildare' on page 27 originally read at his grave in Glasnevin on the centenary of his death, 8 June 1989. Published in Desmond Egan, Hopeful Hopkins, Essays. Goldsmith, 2017.

Father Browne prints are available from Davison and Associates
www.fatherbrowne.com

Archival Material, Hopkins: Irish Jesuit Archives

The publishers would like to thank the following
for their invaluable assistance in the production of this book:
Edwin Davison, Davison Photographic; Damien Burke, Irish Jesuit Archives;
Eddie O'Donnell SJ, former curator of the Father Browne SJ Collection

ISBN 978 1 910248 82 9

Designed by Messenger Publications Design Department
Typeset in Nicolas Cochin, Cochin & Belwe
Printed by Hussar Books

Messenger Publications,
37 Lower Leeson Street, Dublin D02 W938
www.messenger.ie

Gerard Manley
Hopkins SJ
1844~1889

Francis Browne SJ
1880~1960

Preface

Accompanying the author's commentaries and Hopkins's poems is a selection from the photography of the distinguished Jesuit, Fr Frank Browne, who was nine years old when Hopkins died in 1889. The record of buildings in these photographs evokes for us the realities and atmosphere of the Victorian period to which the poet belonged, while the landscapes and seascapes were beloved of both poet and photographer, with the latter frequently following in the footsteps of the former.

One might think that the English convert and the Irish-born Catholic had little in common. Hopkins was a poor preacher, with bad health, and tended towards introversion and depression. Browne was the opposite, on all counts. They shared, however, a similar philosophy of life: a love of nature in all its manifestations, a shared appreciation of the after-life, an unquenchable faith and a pride in being members of 'Christ's Company', both becoming Jesuits. While each achieved acclaim early in life – Hopkins was 'The Star of Balliol', the Oxford College, Browne photographed the *Titanic* – they had to wait for due recognition of their art. Hopkins was helped in achieving this recognition by his friend, Robert Bridges, who published the first collection of Hopkins's poems in 1918. Browne's recognition came when his photographs gradually attained renown following the discovery of all 46,000 of his negatives, twenty-six years after his death, by Eddie O'Donnell SJ.

Both Hopkins and Browne were men of energy and artists of distinction, each in his own medium. In both, the 'heart in hiding stirred'. It 'stirred' in the poet for the inscapes of things as records of the ever-present showings of the divine, and this he expressed with words; it 'stirred', in the more extrovert photographer, the desire to record for the future, by marvel of his eye and camera, how history is shaped by events both big and small.

Contents

Gerard Manley Hopkins

A Life

Gerard Manley Hopkins was born on 28 July 1844 to a refined and artistic Church of England family in the village of Stratford outside London. He was the first of Manley and Kate Hopkins's nine children, and as the family increased in size they moved to Hampstead, a leafy and fashionable suburb north of London. When Hopkins was ten he was enrolled in Highgate, a private school nearby. He came to dislike the school because of the intransigence of the headmaster with whom he had frequent altercations, the most serious of which occurred when the headmaster refused to recommend Hopkins, one of his more brilliant students, for an Oxford scholarship.

Hopkins was quite popular with the other boys at the school. His classmates remember him as being full of fun, rippling with jokes, gifted at rhyming and drawing cartoons. This mischievous side of his nature never left him – in later life it was spoken of as his 'eccentricity'. There were other sides to him too. On hearing stories of the deprivation suffered by sailors out at sea, he gave up all liquids for a week in sympathy. He loved natural beauty. Hampstead at that time was a heath of gorse and broom bushes where sheep grazed, and he liked to take the longer path, edged by hedgerows and oak trees, on his way to school. He was remarkably small and lightly built, and was known to climb the tallest trees to get the best view. The conflicting ideals of love of sensuous abundance, as expressed in his award-winning Highgate poetry, and the ideal of heroic self-sacrifice were already there in the young boy. In

Hopkins' signed Vulgate (Latin Bible), recording the date he was received by Newman into the Catholic faith. Here he has written 31 October, but in fact it was 21 October, 1866.

the adult, priest and poet, they were to become an uneasy mixture. Both would make him the great poet that he became.

Despite his headmaster's intransigence, Hopkins was awarded an exhibition (scholarship) at Balliol College, Oxford, to read Classics, and he moved there in 1863 to begin one of the happy periods of his life. It was rumoured that Benjamin Jowett, Master of Balliol and Hopkins's primary tutor, credited him with being the 'Star of Balliol'. Stardom aside, there were many other things happening in the young poet's life. In the charmingly beautiful university city he was later to describe in 'Duns Scotus's Oxford', he was making friends from many walks of life, some free-thinking, some given to the new science like himself, and some religious and High Church, also like himself. In those days of many friends, one of special importance to him was Robert Bridges, a medical doctor, poet and critic, who would be the chief reader of Hopkins's verse during the poet's lifetime, a collector of his manuscripts and the publisher of his first collection of poems in 1918.

In those days all Oxford students were expected to take an examination in divinity before graduation, to attend evening prayer each day and communion on Sundays, and to avail of a conversation with a father confessor. Hopkins's confessor was the theologian and celebrated preacher, Henry Liddon, who was involved in the Oxford Movement, or Tractarianism, which hoped to renew the Anglican Church by returning it to its origins. Hopkins found his métier in this movement, for he was not enamoured of the Broad Church Anglicanism of Balliol. Through Tractarianism he came to know John Henry Newman, one of its founders, and entrusted to him his long-held desire to become a Catholic. It was a time of yearning, of faith mixed with doubt, and we find it expressed in some of the poems he wrote during this time. Lifting the title 'Heaven-Haven' from a line by one of his favourite poets, seventeenth-century Anglican priest George Herbert, he places it in the mouth of a young nun about to take the veil, and with whom he identifies:

> I have desired to go
> Where springs not fail
> To fields where flies no sharp and sided hail
> And a few lilies blow.
>
> And I have asked to be
> Where no storms come,
> Where the green swell is in the havens dumb,
> And out of the swing of the sea.

This pearl-like poem expresses his desire for the peace of a final decision. But the journey was not easy. Where is God? he asks in 'My prayers must meet a brazen heaven', and in the long poem 'Nondum' (the epigraph of which is from Isaiah 14:15: 'Truly you are a God who hidest Thyself') he accuses God:

> And Thou are silent whilst Thy world
> Contends about its many creeds …

There were objections to his conversion from his family, heightened by the fact that their impulsive son informed them only after making the decision to convert. Like most Anglicans of that time, his father did not have a high opinion of the Catholic Church and begged Henry Liddon to talk sense to his son and save him from throwing away a pure life and somewhat unusual intellect in the cold limbo that Rome assigned to its English converts. His mother's objection in a letter was a single pleading sentence: 'O Gerard, my darling boy, are you indeed gone from me?'[1] But all this was of no avail. Hopkins once said that if anybody ever became a Catholic because 'two and two are four' he did. His stubborn wilfulness and 'motionable mind' found in Catholicism a stability. His intellectual bent found what it was looking for – a truth that was simply *there, there*, as engaging him beyond vagueness. Thus the reality of God became epitomised for him in the Real Presence of the Eucharist, which he saw as parallel to the Incarnation, and the pledge that life need never be sordid or cast adrift because the divine as Real is there for all and everybody, no matter their station.

Writing to his father on 16 October 1866, he explained that Tractarianism and his own study of Catholicism had led his mind to the 'old church' as 'a system that only wants to be known in order to be loved – its consolations, its marvellous ideal of holiness, the faith and devotion of its children, its multiplicity, its array of saints and martyrs, its consistency and unity, its glowing prayers, the daring majesty of its claims …' and, finally, its devotion to the Passion, for 'those who do not pray to Him in His Passion pray to God but scarcely to Christ'.[2]

On 21 October 1866 Hopkins was received into the Catholic Church by Newman and was invited by him to teach for a while in the Oratory School in Birmingham.

JII/4 (2)

BIRMINGHAM V 56 FE27

751

The Revd G. Hopkins SJ.

85. 86 Stephen's Green

Dublin

Two letters to Hopkins from Newman, one dated 27 February 1885, the other 3 March 1887. "Basically conservative and pro empire, he [Hopkins] worried about the empire's possible fragmentation under Gladstone and did not favour the repeal of the Act of Union. However, attentive always to suffering of any kind, he did not deny that Ireland was neglected and mismanaged by Britain. Writing of these concerns to his mentor, Blessed J. H. Newman, the latter's pointed reply [letter below 3 March 1887] must have rocked the poet: 'If I were an Irishman, I should be [in heart] a rebel'. (From Introduction to the Dark Sonnets, page 91)

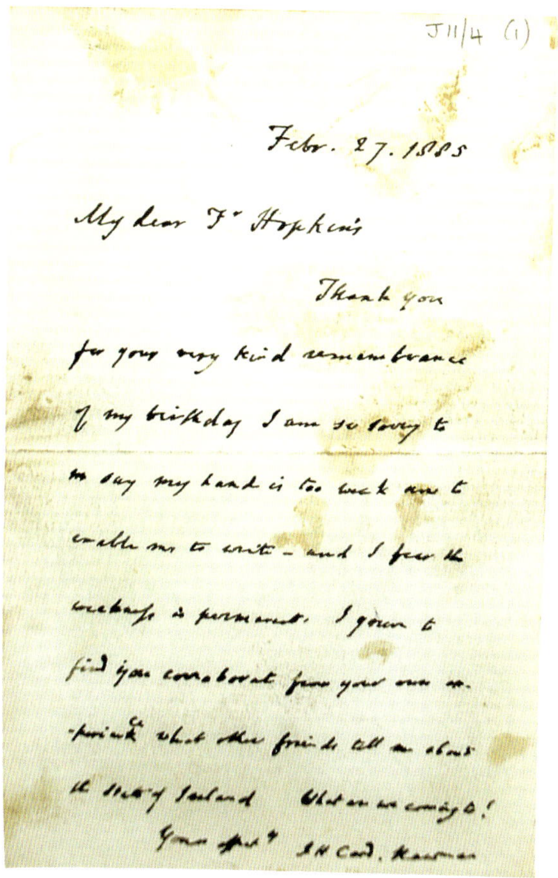
JII/4 (1)

Febr. 27. 1885

My dear Fr Hopkins

Thank you for your very kind remembrance of my birthday. I am so sorry to say my hand is too weak now to enable me to write – and I fear the weakness is permanent. I grieve to find you corroborate from your own experience what other friends tell me about the state of Ireland. What are we coming to!

Yours affect^y J H Card. Newman

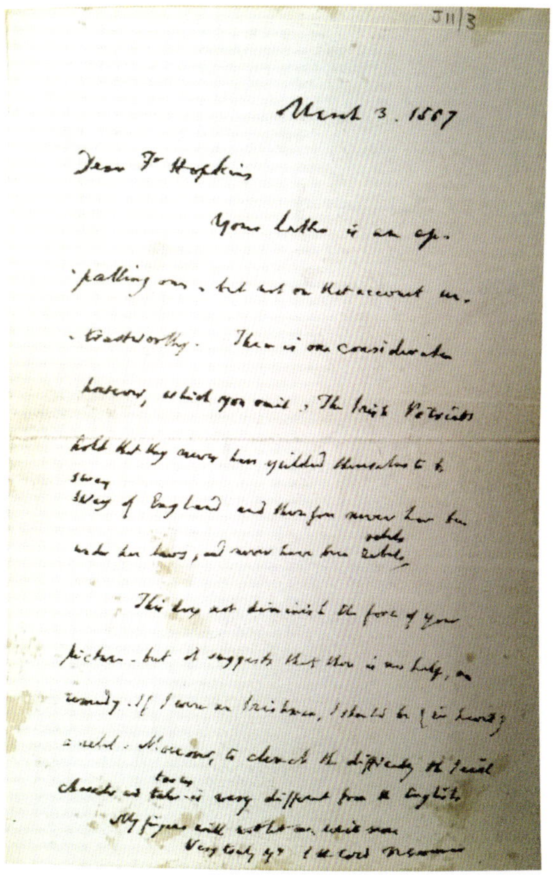
JII/3

March 3. 1887

Dear Fr Hopkins

Your letter is an appalling one – but not on that account untrustworthy. There is one consideration however, which you omit. The Irish Patriots hold that they never have yielded themselves to the sway of England and therefore never have been under her laws, and never have been rebels.

This does not diminish the force of your picture – but it suggests that there is no help, or remedy. If I were an Irishman, I should be (in heart) a rebel. Moreover, to clench the difficulty the Irish character and tastes is very different from the English.

My fingers will not let me write more

Very truly yrs J H Card Newman

But the poet was just marking time, and he spoke to his mentor about his desire to become a priest, either as a Benedictine or a Jesuit. Was there a wisdom in Newman's counsel that the Benedictines would not have suited him, and in his advice not to call Jesuit discipline hard, that it would bring him to heaven? Was the 'heaven' the perceptive Newman had in mind for his protégé not just the salvation of his soul but also the salvation of the immense talent he saw in him, a talent that badly needed discipline if it were to come to fruition?

Making the decision, Hopkins, with characteristic wilfulness, chose to go beyond what was expected of him. On 11 May 1868, he burned all his poems, deciding to give up beauty in his new life until he had leave for it. He called it 'the slaughter of the innocents', but, fortunately, a number of those poems had already been in the possession of family members and Robert Bridges. On 7 September 1868, Hopkins entered the novitiate at Manresa House in Roehampton, London. He wrote no poetry for seven years, and the first poem after that period, 'The Wreck of the Deutschland', written in St Beuno's, Wales, and considered one of his greatest, was begun in December 1875. With this break-through poem came all the sonnets that we know so well today.

Hopkins and Ruskin

A fundamental influence on the poet was the great Victorian aesthete and social critic, John Ruskin. Though not in Oxford during Hopkins's time, his spirit was still there and his *Elements of Drawing* (1857) was popular with aspiring artists. All great art is praise, said Ruskin. It begins with a selfless seeing, 'the innocent eye' which sees nature as it is in itself, the natural world being the eminent tutor of beauty. Ruskin taught that 'if an artist can paint a leaf he can paint the world'. The poet's journals at this time show Ruskin as father to Hopkins's artistic gifts for sketching and word description. 'All my eyes see', he wrote in a later poem.

His word sketches of landscapes are full of details on trees, clouds, the effects of wind movements. These sketches were to be material for his poems. He never

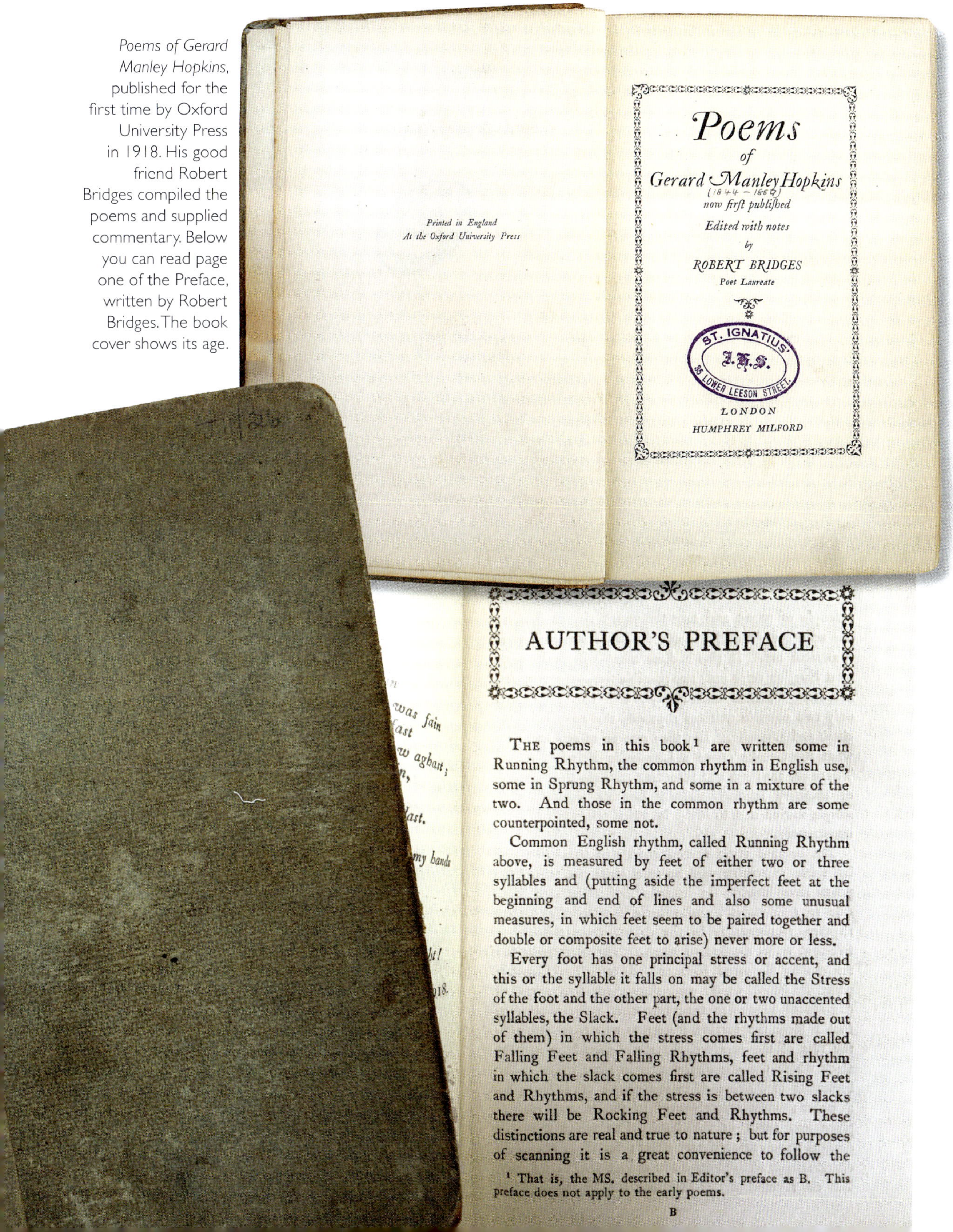

Printed in England
At the Oxford University Press

Poems
of
Gerard Manley Hopkins
(1844 – 1889)
now first published
Edited with notes
by
ROBERT BRIDGES
Poet Laureate

LONDON
HUMPHREY MILFORD

AUTHOR'S PREFACE

THE poems in this book[1] are written some in Running Rhythm, the common rhythm in English use, some in Sprung Rhythm, and some in a mixture of the two. And those in the common rhythm are some counterpointed, some not.

Common English rhythm, called Running Rhythm above, is measured by feet of either two or three syllables and (putting aside the imperfect feet at the beginning and end of lines and also some unusual measures, in which feet seem to be paired together and double or composite feet to arise) never more or less.

Every foot has one principal stress or accent, and this or the syllable it falls on may be called the Stress of the foot and the other part, the one or two unaccented syllables, the Slack. Feet (and the rhythms made out of them) in which the stress comes first are called Falling Feet and Falling Rhythms, feet and rhythm in which the slack comes first are called Rising Feet and Rhythms, and if the stress is between two slacks there will be Rocking Feet and Rhythms. These distinctions are real and true to nature; but for purposes of scanning it is a great convenience to follow the

[1] That is, the MS. described in Editor's preface as B. This preface does not apply to the early poems.

B

Poems of Gerard Manley Hopkins, published for the first time by Oxford University Press in 1918. His good friend Robert Bridges compiled the poems and supplied commentary. Below you can read page one of the Preface, written by Robert Bridges. The book cover shows its age.

romanticised nature by allusions to his moods or feelings. Nature existed out there as a field for passionate observation, replete with a variety of features, forms and selves. We see this in a journal description in May 1871, of an unembarrassed seeing, touching and tasting of bluebells: 'The bluebells in your hand baffle you with their inscape, made to every sense: if you draw you fingers through them they are lodged and struggle with a shock of wet heads; the long stalks rub and click and flatten to a fan on one another like your fingers themselves would when you passed the palms hard across one another, making a brittle rub and jostle like the noise of a hurdle strained by leaning against; then there is the faint honey smell and in the mouth the sweet gum when you bit them. But this is easy, it is the eye they baffle.'[3]

Indeed, Geoffrey Grigson, commenting on the particularising and passionate science of Hopkins, said that to know this poet one must cultivate some equivalence of pure sensation, some of his accurate and emphatic cognition of plants, trees, fruit, skies, clouds, sunsets, birds, waters, surfaces, activities of trades – 'their gear and tackle and trim' – everything which calls to our senses.[4] As Ruskin said, the artist, the aesthete, must first of all learn how to *see*. Hopkins's uncanny single-mindedness in adhering to this dictum helped him shape his own style of poetry. He was not a romantic, and, though an admirer of Wordsworth, he considered that he and other romantic poets were poor observers of nature.

But Ruskin also excited Hopkins at a religious level. He said that to one whose senses are trained, nature is not dense, for true seeing is an engagement of the whole person and leads to an intimate knowing of nature as a Holy Book, with a signic quality. Under Ruskin's indirect influence Hopkins trained his eye for beauty and for particularising description as the way of perceiving it. While such insights from the great Victorian that beauty intuits the divine, and that art is a work of praise, must not be discounted in the poet's formation, the poet desired more certainty intellectually and personally, and later he came to find Ruskin too vague and generic on the relation of God and nature.

Hopkins and the Jesuit Way

A change occurred when Hoplins became a Catholic and moved to living the Catholic way as a Jesuit. The signic quality of Ruskin's vision found what it was searching for in the Christocentric and Incarnational spirituality of Ignatius of Loyola. This was deepened in the poet through the practice of the Jesuit founder's Spiritual Exercises. As he was to write in his retreat notes on 1 January 1889: 'my life is determined by the Incarnation down to most of the details of the day'. He goes on to ask why he shouldn't make it the cause of all he does, more of his especially poetic composition.[5] Thus the Incarnation, the embodiedness of Christ in all things, brought a new 'more' and depth to Hopkins's engagement with the particular and, as we shall see, this was to shape his poetry. As a Jesuit, the Spiritual Exercises encouraged him to relate to the Christ of the Gospels through a sensory and imaginative composition of place and persons. The aim is to make the person of Christ real, so that the Lord is experienced as looking at him and engaging the heart. This validation of 'heart' knowing, with its Ignatian meaning of 'the will' and 'affections', became a source of joy and a new release to the poet. He marvelled at how his personal life, his 'motionable mind' and his heart could be the basis of knowing and action, and that 'heart' and 'tears' could be 'the Mother of being' in him, as we read in 'The Wreck of the Deutschland' (stanza 18).

Group at Clongowes Wood College, County Kildare, c.1885. Back row, left to right: J. Brennan, Anderson, J. Tunney, J. Cahill, J. Kelly, T. Maher, Richard Campbell, Matthew Devitt, Nicholas A. Tomkin, Joseph McDonnell. Front row, left to right; first two standing: John Murphy, James Lynch, Edmund Hogan, Patrick Corcoran, John Conmee (Rector of CWC), John Verdon, Gerard Manley Hopkins.

For this very intellectual poet, the journey to God now expanded to engage the body and the senses, to focus on the particular here and now, and to attend to the special intimacy of *heart* knowledge. The particularism of Ignatius turned that of the poet towards the person of Christ and towards the truth that all things play at Christ by acting out their particular 'selvings', as we read in 'As Kingfishers Catch Fire'. But it was when he turned to Scotus that the Christocentric vision of God in the play of all things became, for him, more intellectually grounded.

Hopkins and Scotus

Duns Scotus was a Franciscan philosopher-theologian who taught at Oxford during the late thirteenth century. Hopkins came across materials by him by chance in the library at Stonyhurst in 1871 and he wrote in his journals that he 'was flushed with a new stroke of enthusiasm. It may come to nothing or it may be a mercy from God. But just then when I took in any inscape of the sky or sea I thought of Scotus'.[6] Hopkins felt confirmed by Scotus in his practice of attending to things in the particularity of their forms. In the charming poem he was to write later, when he was back in Oxford as a priest, 'Duns Scotus's Oxford', the Subtle Doctor is spoken of as the one who 'most sways my spirit to peace; / Of realty the rarest-veined unraveller'.

Scotus's way of knowing reality differed from other medieval schoolmen such as Aquinas, who was the official theologian of the Jesuit order. The Franciscan attached great importance to the individuality and personality of the object known, and said that in the first instance all knowledge is of particulars intuited in their deepest selves in which, when truly seen, are revelations of the whole. The medieval tradition epitomised by Aquinas held that the individual, such as Peter, is really unknowable, and that we only know him through our inherent knowledge of universal human nature as such. According to Scotus, with our intelligence and senses we first come to know Peter as an individual, as *this* human being, not *that* human being. From this concrete knowing of the many Peters, the mind abstracts to the more universal

concept of human nature common to them all. Thus, the reality Scotus gives greatest credence to as the basis of our knowing is the one manifested in *this* Peter, *this* poplar, *this* cloud, *this* sky, *this* blacksmith. Such an apprehension of things is of their *haecceitas*, or *thisness,* and it implies that each created thing or person as *this* contains the whole within itself, and each manifests in its special way the whole as divine presence. For Scotus's view is not of a two-tiered God-world relation, God above and creation below. It is a unity of world in God and God in world in which the Creator is manifested in the diversity and multiplicity of his creatures, and is glorified in the individuality he has willed for them.

I risk this over-simplified summary in order to understand why Hopkins felt confirmed by Scotus. In fact, we find shades of the Subtle Doctor in him even before he read Scotus. In his own mode of unravelling reality, he had coined the words 'inscape' and 'instress'. The inscape (from the Greek root *skopein*, meaning 'to look attentively') is the form or pattern of a thing as it appeals to the senses. It is the very individuality of a thing or person; it touches on its particular truth, its selfhood, and so it touches on beauty. According to Hopkins, getting the inscape is the very soul of art, but he is saddened by the fact that so many people miss the inscape of things, either because they do not take time to see, to hear or to touch, and they move to an abstract universalising knowledge too quickly.

I suspect Hopkins found space in the world view of the Franciscan. He had no problem with the fact that the theologian was considered odd and a maverick by the schoolmen. He believed that if his own poems were to create something new, they would for a time be heard as odd. He defends this in an explanatory letter to Robert Bridges, who found his friend's compositions startling: 'No doubt my poetry errs on the side of being odd … . But as air, melody is what most strikes me in music and design in painting, so design, pattern or what I am in the habit of calling inscape is what I, above all, aim at in poetry'.[7]

There is also the other Hopkins word, 'instress'. If inscape is *what* the poet searches for in things, then instress is *how* it is intuited or experienced. Instress is the universe in communication with us and flooding the whole person. It is helpful to our understanding here to make a comparison between inscape-instress and Word-Spirit in the Christian tradition. It is through the Word of God that we can inscape the truth of who Jesus of Nazareth is, but it is the Spirit of God, as St Paul tells us, that enables us to say, 'Jesus is Lord' (1 Cor 12:3). It is the Holy Spirit who instresses in us the full truth of who Jesus is as the Christ. But Hopkins says there is nothing mechanical or predictable about the relationship of inscape to instress. We are reminded of this in the lovely fifth stanza of 'The Wreck of the Deutschland'. Following on the previous stanzas, it reads like an experience of consolation for the poet. He is looking west through the Clwyd Valley to the Snowdonia range beyond and is instressed by their beauty. As we read on we learn that not only is the divine instress a free gift not to be commanded, it also makes demands on us. On receiving it, the earnest poet says we too must *stress* it, own it in our lives and bring it to others. Because it is something we cannot command, it is felt either as a gift or an absence, which we must bless and understand.

We note that in stanza 6 of 'The Wreck of the Deutschland' the poet asks what, ultimately, is the divine instress in the world. What is it that 'rides time like riding a river'? In stanza 7, he initiates the answer in a simple ballad form:

> It dates from day
> Of his going in Galilee;
> Warm-laid grave of a womb-life grey;
> Manger, maiden's knee …

The answer is the divine event of Incarnation. We know that the spirituality of Incarnation was deepened in the poet by the Ignatian practice of 'God in all things'. In Scotus he found theological confirmation for the intimate connection between creation and Incarnation. Scotus held that the Incarnation was the intentional act of divine love shaping creation from the beginning, and that Christ is the blueprint for all creation. Such insight freed Hopkins to say Christ is inscaped in all creation, in the elements of matter, in all living things, however humble, and in the most highly pitched of creation, the human person. All beings manifest Christ, each in their own way, or, if we stay with the poet's words – and he likes 'action' words – all things are selves that *go* Christ and *speak* Christ, each in their own way (cf. 'As Kingfishers Catch Fire').

A Sacramental Poetry

Promoting Incarnation as a poet meant wording all things by him 'that present and past, / Heaven and earth are word of, worded by' ('The Wreck of the Deutschland', stanza 29). Hopkins never used the word 'sacrament' of his poetry, but there is a consensus among scholars today that he is a sacramental poet. Poems such as 'Pied Beauty' or 'God's Grandeur' are not just windows through which we might look to a divine presence beyond. They are lighted lamps or sacraments that attempt to hold the presence they signify.

As sacramental, Hopkins's poetic style does not symbolise. His is a language of mimesis. He descriptively mimes the contours of Incarnation in the world in its inner and outer meanings, and he wakes us up to its showings in the universe. He never takes his eyes off the universe and uses images rather than ideas to tell of God's presence in the world. His is not a two-tiered universe of God above and creation below. In line with Scotus, the Creator, the biblical I AM, though different in pitch from created things, is one *realty* with created things, and to believe is to assent to this divine *thisness*. For this certitude, so important to him, he found a basis in Parmenides, a Greek philosopher of the fifth and sixth century BC. In 1868 he wrote, 'I have often felt when I have been in this mood and felt the depth of an instress or how fast the inscape holds a thing that nothing is so pregnant and straightforward to the truth as simple *yes* and *is*'.[8]

There is but one reality for Hopkins – of God in the world and the world in the biblical I AM. R. K. R. Thornton aptly sums it up when he writes: Hopkins can only write about one thing: 'Everything IS; and everything is Christ'.[9] For a true reading of many of his poems we have to submit selflessly to this given reality in them and say our *yes* and *it is*.

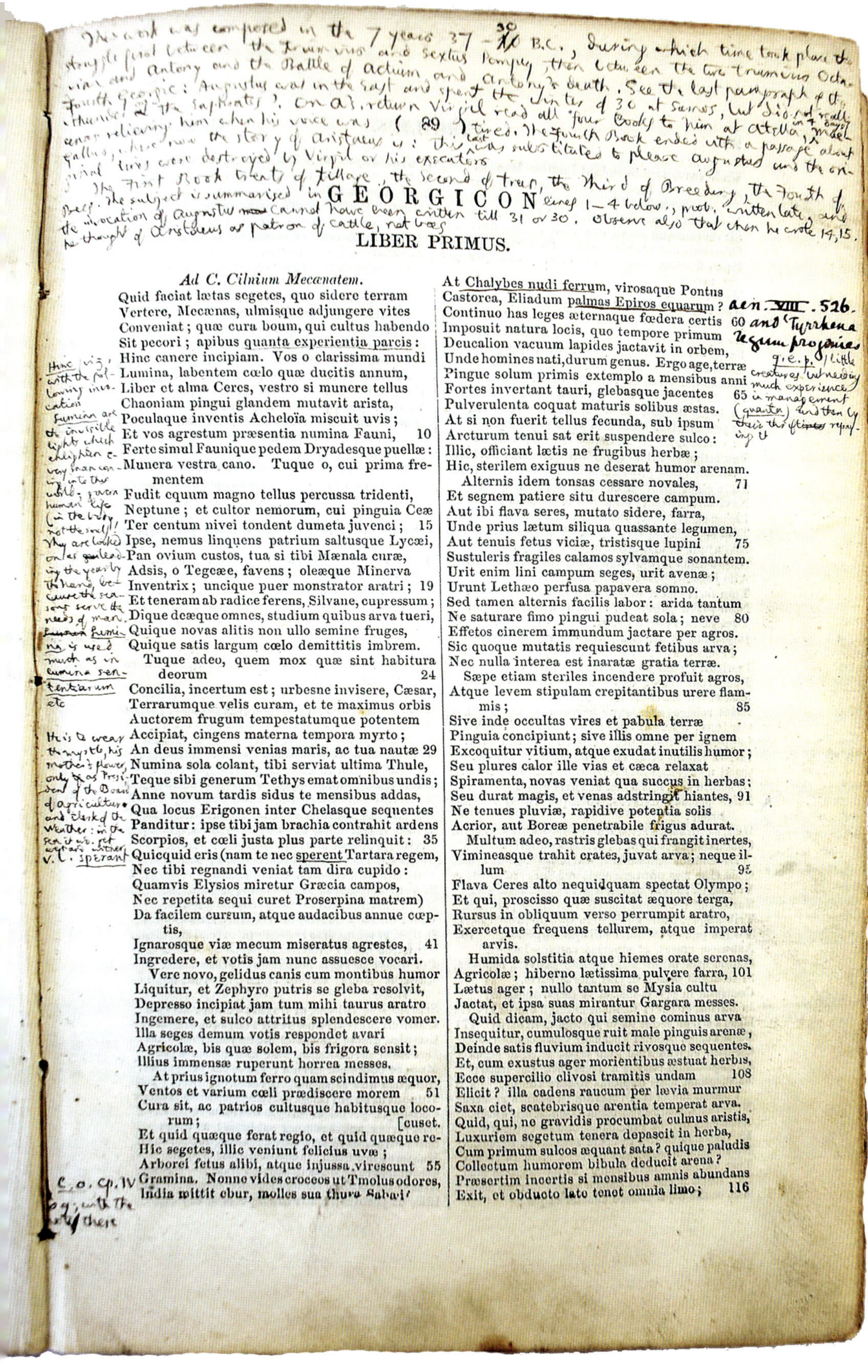

GEORGICON

LIBER PRIMUS.

Ad C. Cilnium Mecœnatem.

Quid faciat lætas segetes, quo sidere terram
Vertere, Mecœnas, ulmisque adjungere vites
Conveniat; quæ cura boum, qui cultus habendo
Sit pecori; apibus quanta experientia parcis:
Hinc canere incipiam. Vos o clarissima mundi
Lumina, labentem cœlo quæ ducitis annum,
Liber et alma Ceres, vestro si munere tellus
Chaoniam pingui glandem mutavit arista,
Poculaque inventis Acheloïa miscuit uvis;
Et vos agrestum præsentia numina Fauni,
Ferte simul Faunique pedem Dryadesque puellæ:
Munera vestra cano. Tuque o, cui prima frementem
Fudit equum magno tellus percussa tridenti,
Neptune; et cultor nemorum, cui pinguia Ceæ
Ter centum nivei tondent dumeta juvenci;
Ipse, nemus linquens patrium saltusque Lycæi,
Pan ovium custos, tua si tibi Mænala curæ,
Adsis, o Tegeæe, favens; oleæque Minerva
Inventrix; uncique puer monstrator aratri;
Et teneram ab radice ferens, Silvane, cupressum;
Dique deæque omnes, studium quibus arva tueri,
Quique novas alitis non ullo semine fruges,
Quique satis largum cœlo demittitis imbrem.
Tuque adeo, quem mox quæ sint habitura deorum
Concilia, incertum est; urbesne invisere, Cæsar,
Terrarumque velis curam, et te maximus orbis
Auctorem frugum tempestatumque potentem
Accipiat, cingens materna tempora myrto;
An deus immensi venias maris, ac tua nautæ
Numina sola colant, tibi serviat ultima Thule,
Teque sibi generum Tethys emat omnibus undis;
Anne novum tardis sidus te mensibus addas,
Qua locus Erigonen inter Chelasque sequentes
Panditur: ipse tibi jam brachia contrahit ardens
Scorpios, et cœli justa plus parte relinquit:
Quicquid eris (nam te nec sperent Tartara regem,
Nec tibi regnandi veniat tam dira cupido:
Quamvis Elysios miretur Græcia campos,
Nec repetita sequi curet Proserpina matrem)
Da facilem cursum, atque audacibus annue cœptis,
Ignarosque viæ mecum miseratus agrestes,
Ingredere, et votis jam nunc assuesce vocari.
Vere novo, gelidus canis cum montibus humor
Liquitur, et Zephyro putris se gleba resolvit,
Depresso incipiat jam tum mihi taurus aratro
Ingemere, et sulco attritus splendescere vomer.
Illa seges demum votis respondet avari
Agricolæ, bis quæ solem, bis frigora sensit;
Illius immensæ ruperunt horrea messes.
At prius ignotum ferro quam scindimus æquor,
Ventos et varium cœli prædiscere morem
Cura sit, ac patrios cultusque habitusque locorum;
Et quid quæque ferat regio, et quid quæque recuset.
Hic segetes, illic veniunt felicius uvæ;
Arborei fetus alibi, atque injussa virescunt
Gramina. Nonne vides croceos ut Tmolus odores,
India mittit ebur, molles sua thura Sabæi;
At Chalybes nudi ferrum, virosaque Pontus
Castorea, Eliadum palmas Epiros equarum?
Continuo has leges æternaque fœdera certis
Imposuit natura locis, quo tempore primum
Deucalion vacuum lapides jactavit in orbem,
Unde homines nati, durum genus. Ergo age, terræ
Pingue solum primis extemplo a mensibus anni
Fortes invertant tauri, glebasque jacentes
Pulverulenta coquat maturis solibus æstas.
At si non fuerit tellus fecunda, sub ipsum
Arcturum tenui sat erit suspendere sulco:
Illic, officiant lætis ne frugibus herbæ;
Hic, sterilem exiguus ne deserat humor arenam.
Alternis idem tonsas cessare novales,
Et segnem patiere situ durescere campum.
Aut ibi flava seres, mutato sidere, farra,
Unde prius lætum siliqua quassante legumen,
Aut tenuis fetus viciæ, tristisque lupini
Sustuleris fragiles calamos sylvamque sonantem.
Urit enim lini campum seges, urit avenæ;
Urunt Lethæo perfusa papavera somno.
Sed tamen alternis facilis labor: arida tantum
Ne saturare fimo pingui pudeat sola; neve
Effetos cinerem immundum jactare per agros.
Sic quoque mutatis requiescunt fetibus arva;
Nec nulla interea est inaratæ gratia terræ.
Sæpe etiam steriles incendere profuit agros,
Atque levem stipulam crepitantibus urere flammis;
Sive inde occultas vires et pabula terræ
Pinguia concipiunt; sive illis omne per ignem
Excoquitur vitium, atque exudat inutilis humor;
Seu plures calor ille vias et cæca relaxat
Spiramenta, novas veniat qua succus in herbas;
Seu durat magis, et venas adstringit hiantes,
Ne tenues pluviæ, rapidive potentia solis
Acrior, aut Boreæ penetrabile frigus adurat.
Multum adeo, rastris glebas qui frangit inertes,
Vimineasque trahit crates, juvat arva; neque illum
Flava Ceres alto nequidquam spectat Olympo;
Et qui, proscisso quæ suscitat æquore terga,
Rursus in obliquum verso perrumpit aratro,
Exercetque frequens tellurem, atque imperat arvis.
Humida solstitia atque hiemes orate serenas,
Agricolæ; hiberno lætissima pulvere farra,
Lætus ager; nullo tantum se Mysia cultu
Jactat, et ipsa suas mirantur Gargara messes.
Quid dicam, jacto qui semine cominus arva
Insequitur, cumulosque ruit male pinguis arenæ,
Deinde satis fluvium inducit rivosque sequentes.
Et, cum exustus ager morientibus æstuat herbis,
Ecce supercilio clivosi tramitis undam
Elicit? illa cadens raucum per lævia murmur
Saxa ciet, scatebrisque arentia temperat arva.
Quid, qui, ne gravidis procumbat culmus aristis,
Luxuriem segetum tenera depascit in herba,
Cum primum sulcos æquant sata? quique paludis
Collectum humorem bibula deducit arena?
Præsertim incertis si mensibus amnis abundans
Exit, et obducto late tenet omnia limo;

Corpus Poetarum Latinorum by William S Walker (ed) London, 1878. Annotations by Gerard Manley Hopkins are an example of his minute attention to textual details. This book was used by him to teach at University College, Dublin.

POEMS 1876–1889

THE WRECK OF THE DEUTSCHLAND

To the
happy memory of five Franciscan Nuns
exiles by the Falk Laws
drowned between midnight and morning of
Dec. 7th. 1875

PART THE FIRST

I

Thou mastering me
God! giver of breath and bread;
World's strand, sway of the sea;
Lord of living and dead;
Thou hast bound bones and veins in me, fastened me flesh,
And after it almost unmade, what with dread,
Thy doing: and dost thou touch me afresh?
Over again I feel thy finger and find thee.

Despite this 'one thing' Hopkins is never boring. His one thing – the *it is*, the Christ inscaped in all things – is elaborated on variously by his use of language. As a poet, he believed that the language of poetry should be the current language of the age, heightened, and unlike itself. He uses a sprung rhythm – where lines borrow beats from the next line – therefore irregularly accented like the spoken word, yet not irregular in the sense of free-wheeling verse. N. H. MacKenzie says we should think of it like this: it is a springing use of language like 'the natural grace of a deer springing down a mountainside, adjusting the length of each leap according to the ground it is covering'.[10]

Sprung rhythm features greatly in his first great poem 'The Wreck of the Deutschland'. Hopkins wrote to Canon Dixon, a longtime friend, poet and Anglican priest, who was also a reader of his poetry, saying that the poem gave him the opportunity to try out what long had been haunting his ear, the echo of a new rhythm which he had now realised on paper.[11] Moving beyond the poetic rules of regular or running rhythm, this new rhythm allows him to charge each poetic line with maximum energy, in imitation and praise of what he perceives nature to be, as locus of Incarnation and promise of Resurrection. This brings a forceful quality to his poetry, and the language is quite sinewy, thumping and visceral at times. He uses compounded words; he invents words, he compresses words. His recovers Anglo-Saxon one-syllable nouns, which give a jaggedness to his verse, and which also connote the dapple of 'abrupt selves' with which a Hopkins poem is thronged. In all this we get a sense of the earnestness of the voice who speaks to us, not only that of the poet as man of letters, but that of the priest, desiring to give his readers an experience of the great truth of Incarnation that obsesses him. Thus, language is at the forefront of a Hopkins poem. He advises readers to read his poetry for its rhythm and musicality, for these are part of the inscape of the poem which fully reveals itself in time. And so, his poetry has a freshness of style that invites the reader to come to it again and again.

First page of *The Wreck of the Deutschland* from Hopkins's own book of poems pictured on page 15

Being in St Beuno's for a few months deepened my interest in Hopkins. I walked his roads, upper and lower, took in his 'loveable west' and how the Vale of Clwyd carries the eyes to Snowdonia. But when I gave him more attention I realised that as well as being a nature poet, he is also deeply religious in the Christian sense. This mattered to me because I have been teaching theology at various levels for most of my working life. Long ago as a student I poured over Aquinas's *Summa Theologica*, much of which was beyond me at that time, yet felt a certain warmth in my heart as I revelled in the clarity of St Thomas's thought system. A text from a Greek Father, St Gregory Nazianzen, kept me going at that time. Writing of the importance of perseverance in study of the things of God, Gregory went on to say: 'Knowledge becomes love when the known is of its nature beautiful.' I have always cherished that text and the truth that theology and faith are about the beautiful as much as they are about truth (and reason) and the good (the moral life).

In fact, without beauty Christian truth may become a system of logical correctness and the faith we believe in, a jumble of creeds. Without beauty the practice of the good may end up in selfishness. We need a vision that brings beauty back to faith, and this is what Hopkins does. He does it in his own signature way with a refreshing realism. For beauty is not just an idea but the felt illumination of particular things in their inscapes. It is *this* beauty and *that* beauty. Hopkins conveys that the realism of Christian truth means it is not a vague object of spiritual our seeking that we never reach. It is given; *it is.* 'Everything IS and everything is Christ.' Given to us to be encountered, it requires our *yes* and *it is*, just as our being in the world of things and persons requires *yes* and *it is*. The beauty of things and persons 'keeps warm / Men's wits to the things that are'. It engages us. It is the truth and goodness of God who is, 'Beauty's self and beauty's giver' in touch with us.

And so the poet says, beauty *bids* us – another Hopkins word. Beauty moves us, requires us to give, to change, as he himself is moved to change, to practise 'patience, prayer, alms', as he is called to by the beauty of a Starlight Night.

In the commentaries we will see more of the biography of the poet. The biographies I draw upon are of help here. His spiritual and devotional writings and his letters tell of the struggles of the priest-poet and the cost to him of the hard-won insights he transmuted into verse. Taking time to know him in this way is rewarding. We bring him – this very English poet – out of the nineteenth century to make him ours. We come to love him and want to thank him for all he has left us. In early May 1889, Hopkins fell ill and was diagnosed with a strain of typhoid fever. On the night of 5 June, he took a turn for the worse, and his parents were called. He asked for the Viaticum when he knew he was dying, and received it for the last time on the morning of 8 June. According to the members of the college community, he was heard two or three times before he died to say, 'I am so happy, I am so happy.' He is buried in the plot owned by the Jesuits in Dublin's Glasnevin Cemetery. I leave you with this extract from a poem composed by Irish poet Desmond Egan, who has a poet's understanding of Hopkins and an obvious affection for him. He expresses our thanks. The entire poem was read by Egan at Hopkins' grave on the centenary of the poet's death, 8 June 1989:

> and through lines you will us we may glimpse
> a face gone pale with thinking
> a head too large
> for a build slight as Beckett's
> the English fingers the unreachable
> melancholy of the artist
> as we converge in tribute to you
> our more than friend our dear relation
> and to your convert's almost medieval search for
> certainties none of us dare to expect
> since we are all *time's eunuchs*
> although you broke into wholeness at the end
> and died like Simeon so happy.[12]

Gerardo M. Hopkins S.J.

The Poems

The following commentaries on Hopkins's works may offer alternative insights to those who already know him. I recommend them especially to beginning readers or for use by a poetry group who wish to study the poet together. While offering clarity where needed, the commentaries are also meant to be a stimulus for your own responses. There are many opinions on Hopkins and I think that is what the poet would like.

The poems I select are broadly from three periods of his life:

(i) The Welsh period when he lived in St Beuno's in North Wales: Salad Days

(ii) The period of ministry in various places as a priest: Fortune's Football

(iii) The Dublin period until his death on 8 June 1889, selection from the Dark Sonnets and other poems: The Times Are Nightfall

'The Wreck of the Deutschland', his first major work, I have left to the end. Reading it later, having a sense of the poet's style and concerns, it will be appreciated it as the tour de force it is.

The resources I have recommended are listed in the Bibliography. I recommend especially Walford Davies's commentary, a small book, but a great companion for studying the poet. His commentary avoids analysing Hopkins' poetry – this one finds in the excellent introduction – and focusses on the language used. Hopkins does say he needs explanation. Attending to language is a necessary first step, and facilitates enjoyment of the poems.

Panorama with farmer at work, Llandudno, Wales, 1947

Part One

THE SALAD DAYS

St Beuno's, North Wales

Looking back at South Stack from SS Scotia, Holyhead, Gwynedd, Wales, August 1937

God's Grandeur

THIS IS one of Hopkins's most popular and well known poems. With this first of the ten sonnets he wrote during his Welsh period, his 'salad days', the Hopkins world opens before us. As in musical composition he liked a form or structure within which to work. In the sonnet form we have the octave, in which the poet lays out his wares, and the sestet, in which he addresses the deeper meaning. These poems, these 'airy cages' (Walford Davies), draw us at the level of the senses and observation. His poetry is 'a passionate science'. What he wants to communicate is given to us when we see, hear and touch the universe that is there for us.

Hopkins was always a close observer of nature. He kept sketches and notes of his walks and believed that one could only truly see and hear when alone. A Jesuit brother remembered the scholar 'Mr 'opkins' at Stonyhurst in 1882. 'Ay, a strange young man, crouching down that gate to stare at some wet sand. A fair natural 'e seemed to us.'[13] Like a biblical prophet, he is a voracious exegete of the universe, plumbing for the inscapes that address (instress) him out of the 'thinginess' of creation. In these inscapes he will ultimately detect the dynamic 'more', which also addresses the *ad majorem* (the greater), as he the Jesuit would name it, and which in the poet is Incarnation as divine presence in all things. In this sonnet Incarnation is simply celebrated as 'the grandeur of God'.

Divine grandeur is manifested in two ways – in terms of light and density. The grandeur can reveal itself with lightning rapidity, as in the 'shook foil'. A humble unpoetic image of the glory of God, it might be said, but it is possible that the ever-experimenting poet does not have in mind here the flat dull piece of gold foil, but the same piece, which, when shaken, gives off lightning-like charges. This word 'charge' matters to him. For those who know how to see, the world is 'charged' with the grandeur of God. We also find this dynamic verb in his devotional writings. 'All things, therefore, are charged with love, are charged with God, if we know how to touch them, give off sparks and take fire, yield drops and flow, ring and tell of him'.[14] But meanings are always multiple with Hopkins, and the recent invention of electricity with its notion of high voltage would have validated his view that the active grandeur of God in the universe is showing itself in this gift too. However, he is realistic: the glory may also ask more of us over time. '[Like the ooze of oil / Crushed', it may call us to suffer in some way so that we may participate in the redemptive divine suffering in our world. Whichever it is, we need to hear that the divine grandeur in the world is a *charge* put upon us. If we do 'not reck his rod' of authority, or heed his cross (Old English 'rood'), we will obliterate the variety of our universe and ourselves with it. With the sonorous flatness of 'seared', 'bleared, smeared', the poet is aware that outside the beauty of the valley in which he wrote this poem, Wales itself had numerous areas blighted by the fallout of the Industrial Revolution in nineteenth-century Britain.

The sonnet comes to some resolution in the final sestet. We can trust 'the dearest freshness deep down things'. Yet, as always with Hopkins, 'dearest' has another possible meaning – costly – and 'black West' can refer to the coal mines and smelting works and the 'smudge' of industry. However, there is hope, for the bleak earth is not without the nurture of the feminine aspect of the Creator through the warm brooding of the Holy Spirit who does not desert it. The biblical overtones of this poem are plentiful and it may be read in conjunction with Psalm 18. It is the doorway to the other sonnets, all of which must be read, if we are to understand Hopkins, with what St Augustine calls *fides osculata* – the faith 'that has eyes'.[15]

God's Grandeur

The world is charged with the grandeur of God.
   It will flame out, like shining from shook foil;
   It gathers to a greatness, like the ooze of oil
Crushed. Why do men then now not reck his rod?
Generations have trod, have trod, have trod;
   And all is seared with trade; bleared, smeared with toil;
   And wears man's smudge and shares man's smell: the soil
Is bare now, nor can foot feel, being shod.

And for all this, nature is never spent;
   There lives the dearest freshness deep down things;
And though the last lights off the black West went
   Oh, morning, at the brown brink eastward, springs—
Because the Holy Ghost over the bent
   World broods with warm breast and with ah! bright wings.

The Starlight Night

THIS POEM is a cousin of the later 'Hurrahing in Harvest' in which, in September 1877, walking through a harvest field, Hopkins looks up and proactively gleans our Saviour in the heavens. Christ is always there as given to us in all things, but sometimes the 'earnest' poet takes on the search for Christ as a conscious task. In this poem, as in the later one, he does this. In the poem we have to raise ourselves up to participate consciously in an imaginative leap with the poet.

Written on 24 February 1877, the poem's immediate inspiration was a clear and starry night in North Wales. Hopkins looks up a lot. We get a sense of impulse and delight as we are instructed to look up four times – there are fourteen exclamation marks! It is a poem of pure imagination, in that we are invited into the myth he creates of an alternative sky world of stars as people, living in medieval walled burrows, each defended by a citadel. Then, in line 4, with a further leap of imagination, he asks us to look down upon a redeemed world. What kind of world? A busy world, varied, ordered, full of movement and beautiful. In the dim woods the pits ('delves') of diamonds sparkle like the eyes of the busy elves who mine them. The cold dawn landscape catches the flare of the stars as the 'whitebeam' (chess apple with white blossoms) and the 'abeles' (tall poplars), showing the underside of their leaves, act like a scare of farmyard birds. So much beauty! Hopkins is overwhelmed: What must we do? he asks. 'Buy then! bid then!' 'Bid' and 'bidding' mean a great deal to the poet. He sees his poetry as addressing the listener, and he commands the listener's response with words like 'look', 'pray', 'buy', 'bid'. In this poem we are asked to 'bid' for the beauty of the starry night with 'Prayer, patience, alms, vows'.

In patience and prayer we discover we are bidding for more. What is the 'more'? Lacking words to express it directly, and possibly, as a poet, not wishing to do so, he moves into his topic and says it slant, as Emily Dickinson would say. He turns to the

Springtime in the Grapery, Emo, 1931

natural world, to the lighted white clusters of stars like May blossoms; they remind him of the March catkins hanging from the willow trees with yellow meal or dust on their furry coats. Again, a whole spectrum of possible meanings streams through his words here, as he focuses on the word 'meal'. The meal is the shocks or sheaves all set out in the barn where the harvest of the redeemer, Christ (Mt 13:30), is gathered. This is the 'more'. This is what we go home to. The source of all beauty in the world, it is where we will find the banquet with Christ, his mother and all his saints.

Be prepared to travel with this poem from earth to heaven and from heaven back to transformed earth. It is truly a Scotistic experience, which implies that the creation of the universe and all its creatures is a field for Christ's action. Despite his theological language, Hopkins is quite a this-worldly poet. Because of Incarnation, it is on earth, among the everyday trivia that we glean the Saviour. I dare say he would agree with Robert Frost's axiom from 'Birches': 'Earth's the right place for love: / I don't know where it is likely to go better.'

The Starlight Night

Look at the stars! look, look up at the skies!
 O look at all the fire-folk sitting in the air!
 The bright boroughs, the circle-citadels there!
Down in dim woods the diamond delves! the elves'-eyes!
The grey lawns cold where gold, where quickgold lies!
 Wind-beat whitebeam! airy abeles set on a flare!
 Flake-doves sent floating forth at a farmyard scare!—
Ah well! it is all a purchase, all is a prize.
Buy then! bid then!—What?—Prayer, patience, aims, vows.
Look, look: a May-mess, like on orchard boughs!
 Look! March-bloom, like on mealed-with-yellow sallows!
These are indeed the barn; withindoors house
The shocks. This piece-bright paling shuts the spouse
 Christ home, Christ and his mother and all his hallows.

Pied Beauty

THIS POEM was written in the village of Tremerchion near St Beuno's in summer 1887, after the final exams. Hopkins later informs Robert Bridges that he will not be staying on for a fourth year and that, sadly, he will have to leave Wales and the 'loveable west'. This unusual curtailed sonnet of six lines and four, was originally framed by the Jesuit mottoes 'For the Greater Glory of God' (*Ad Majorem Dei Gloriam*) and 'Praise to God Always' (*Laus Deo Semper*), which were later absorbed into the text. It is a poem of display. Knowing he is leaving, the poet lets it rip! This is not one of his priestly poems; he does not 'bid' the reader to change in any way. He is quite free and unconventional and God is also unconventional. As the artist Creator, God is Beauty and divine beauty shows itself as variegated and 'dappled'. It is 'counter', 'original', 'spare', 'strange'. Varied and full of thinginess, it is this beauty and that beauty and it appeals to all our senses.

This multiplicity and dapple are also aspects of the glory, the grandeur of God, which in this poem shows itself as a divine expansiveness. In the first stanza, with the bunching together of nouns, Hopkins invites us not only to see the colours but to touch and feel the textures. It is a rich universe. He lists his data in parallels as in the Psalms (see Psalm 148), and the text invites a contemplative circling around and a return to what is simply there before our eyes. You simply look, says the poet, at what looks back at you. No need to ask questions. Does the poet flippantly dismiss a question in line 2 of the last stanza? Yet any anxiety or fear that the multifaceted universe is an atomistic or groundless one is assuaged by the last line. The Creator-Father is an unchanging real presence. The Absolute Beauty holds all things together and we can give praise.

Pied Beauty

Glory be to God for dappled things—
 For skies of couple-colour as a brinded cow;
  For rose-moles all in stipple upon trout that swim;
Fresh-firecoal chestnut-falls; finches' wings;
 Landscape plotted and pieced—fold, fallow, and plough;
  And all trades, their gear and tackle and trim.

All things counter, original, spare, strange;
 Whatever is fickle, freckled (who knows how?)
  With swift, slow; sweet, sour; adazzle, dim;
He fathers-forth whose beauty is past change:
        Praise him.

'As kingfishers catch fire'

'AS KINGFISHERS Catch Fire' is undated, has no title and is never mentioned in letters. It was found among Hopkins's papers after his death. However, as it has all the verve and freshness of the St Beuno's sonnets, I am presenting it here, guided by N. H. MacKenzie, as a sonnet of this Welsh period. It is a valuable poem, for in it we find the clearest synthesis of Hopkins's aesthetic and religious world view – there is the simple 'yes' to what *is* in all its singularity and diversity. Of course there is also the Scotus-Hopkins understanding of the universe as manifesting itself in the 'thisness' of things. The poet goes further and tells us the 'being indoors each one dwells' is a *self*, a self as action, crying out its name and communicating its 'self' to us. We are part of this selving and going universe too. We open our eyes and ears and see and hear many levels of selving – the ring of stones tumbled into 'roundy wells', the special sound of bells, some of which have a name, such as Great Tom of Christchurch, Oxford, which Hopkins would have been aware of, and the flaming out of light and colour from the kingfisher, Britain's most splendid bird, and from the more evanescent dragonflies, of which there are forty species in the country.

When Hopkins comes specifically to the human in the sestet, however, he says 'I say more'. Indeed, there is always 'more' in a Hopkins poem. It is up to the reader to find it. And the 'more' is not an added-on tier that we might dispense with. It is integral to the poet's Christian belief that the universe itself is the place of selving of the divine, since the human form and face of this divine selving in all things is Christ. In January 1889, Hopkins wrote in his retreat notes: 'My life is determined by the Incarnation down to most of the details of the day'.[16] We can say that his poetry is also determined by the Incarnation. He writes so that his words may embody Christ, and all levels of the universe are of interest to him and provide material for poetry – inanimate things in their beauty and terror, the mortal animate world and, more especially, human beings in their individuating design or 'inscape'. The more these things truly manifest their selving, the more they manifest Christ. This poem is a tutorial on that truth.

'As kingfishers catch fire'

As kingfishers catch fire, dragonflies draw flame;
   As tumbled over rim in roundy wells
   Stones ring; like each tucked string tells, each hung bell's
Bow swung finds tongue to fling out broad its name;
Each mortal thing does one thing and the same:
   Deals out that being indoors each one dwells;
   Selves—goes itself; myself it speaks and spells,
Crying *What I do is me: for that I came.*

I say more: the just man justices;
   Keeps grace: that keeps all his goings graces;
Acts in God's eye what in God's eye he is—
   Christ—for Christ plays in ten thousand places,
Lovely in limbs, and lovely in eyes not his
   To the Father through the features of men's faces.

I conclude with two comments for consideration. The first is that Hopkins's religious vision of the 'more' here is of the redeemed and graced human being who participates in and also contributes to the selving of Christ in the world. It is interesting that the virtue he chooses to characterise this graced selving is *justice.* Is it that justice brings a certain moral astringency to love? From his spiritual writings we glean that the poet is quite a morally concerned person. Love for him is always love in action; it is sacrificial and in service of the other. The second comment is that we note how the play of Christ, 'Lovely in limbs, and lovely in eyes not his', also presages an ecumenism of relationship with multiple *others*, not only the other of the earth on which we live and which calls for our ecological respect, but also the other of peoples and races, their cultures and religions. As a poet he moves beyond the nineteenth-century theology in which he was formed to say what a great ecumenist of our time, the Anglican bishop and Islamic scholar, Kenneth Cragg, has said: 'It takes the whole world to understand the whole Christ.'

The Windhover

HOPKINS speaks of two kinds of 'clearances' in reading poetry: either the meaning is felt without effort as fast as one reads, or else, while a poem can be obscure at first reading, when we work with it patiently, it will explode. 'The Windhover', written on 30 May 1877, 'the best thing I ever wrote', is a poem that explodes. It explodes for a number of reasons. It invites a reading aloud. It is not a poem that I can contain, for it contains me, the reader. We are swept along with the kestrel. With the generous use of imagery and sprung rhythm, the poet gives body to the energy of the bird and the word it speaks to him – no sedate five-beat lines here. Some lines spill over in outrides and steal a beat or beats from the next line. Nouns and adjectives cluster together with assonance. There is the sharp staccato alliteration of consonants, and the poem rises and dips with the movement of the bird.

Noel Maenefa, the dark hillock behind St Beuno's, with its Rock Chapel on top, to which the Jesuit students sometimes went for a special liturgy, was a great haunt of hawks and owls. The kestrel, a small hawk, is 'caught' and held within the poet's attention early one morning. In his mind's eye, he sees the little 'dapple-dawn-drawn' kestrel like a knight riding, akin to the falcon, a favourite minion of the French court. He imagines the bird's motion in the air like the ringing of a bell. We note the ringing quality of the first lines, and can almost anticipate the whirring sound as the kestrel rings upon the air of its wimpling wing. It's as if the windhover is ecstatic in its hurling and gliding and especially in its rebuff of the big wind.

Hopkins is also *caught* by this *rebuff*. He responds: 'My heart in hiding / Stirred for a bird, – the achieve of, the mastery of the thing!' We are jolted here by the use of the word 'thing'. We note in the title that the dedication of this poem is 'To Christ our Lord', but that does not mean that the materiality of things does not matter. A hawk is always a hawk for Hopkins. 'Things' matter because it is in their very 'selving' that they inscape Christ. Not a romantic poet in the Wordsworthian tradition, he does not read nature as an expression of his emotions or as a pointer to or signification of the divine. He reads it sacramentally or incarnationally. As a Catholic, he believes that the enfleshment of the divine has taken place historically in Christ, and because of the Incarnation it is also taking place throughout all levels of nature and within all beings, created as they are to manifest the divine and to give God praise.

The '*I say more*' of Hopkins is never far way when we persist with his poetry. We wonder what he means by the 'heart in hiding'? Is it possible that as a bird-watcher he is restraining any physical impulse that might frighten the bird? Then there is the verb 'stirred'? Is it that he envies the 'achieve' and 'mastery' of the kestrel, a *thing* in its pure natural state, whereas he feels he is not accomplishing anything? Much has been written on the phrase 'my heart in hiding', but it seems to me that the words 'Buckle!' and 'AND' (his capitals) imply that the poet's heart in hiding has become a smitten heart. A transformation has occurred in him. It is in its buckling in the air that he finds the kestrel so much more lovely and dangerous. It is a high moment. With 'AND', he moves on to utter words of relief and affection, indeed of recognition: 'O my chevalier!' For the buckling of the brute nature of the bird is a word for him of another knight who was also lovely and dangerous in his buckling on the Cross.

Indeed, the pivotal 'AND' marks a resolution he plays out in the sestet. 'No wonder of it', he says dismissively, thinking of his own lack of achievement. It may be that a phrase of his mentor, Blessed John Henry Newman, has come to him – 'Nothing is wasted'. The 'sheer plod' of the everyday can generate its own danger and loveliness as the plough does when it makes wet 'sillion' shine, and as the falling of blue-bleak embers in a fire release 'gold-vermillion'.

In the last two lines it is possible to find hints again of the self-emptying of the Passion with words like 'gall', 'gash' and the 'vermillion' of blood. The heartfelt quality of what the poet is experiencing and the peace it brings are expressed with the 'ah my dear' to Christ, the phrase borrowed from George Herbert's lovely poem: 'Love Bade Me Welcome'.

The Windhover

I caught this morning morning's minion, king–
  dom of daylight's dauphin, dapple-dawn-drawn Falcon, in his riding
  Of the rolling level underneath him steady air, and striding
High there, how he rung upon the rein of a wimpling wing
In his ecstasy! then off, off forth on swing,
  As a skate's heel sweeps smooth on a bow-bend: the hurl and gliding
  Rebuffed the big wind. My heart in hiding
Stirred for a bird,—the achieve of; the mastery of the thing!

Brute beauty and valour and act, oh, air, pride, plume, here
  Buckle! AND the fire that breaks from thee then, a billion
Times told lovelier, more dangerous, O my chevalier!

  No wonder of it: sheer plod makes plough down sillion
Shine, and blue-bleak embers, ah my dear,
  Fall, gall themselves, and gash gold-vermillion.

Spring

ONE OF the glories of this poem is in the way it attempts to bring about in its readers the awakening of spring. It was written during the Whitsun holiday weekend in May 1877, while Hopkins was out walking near St Beuno's in North Wales. The poet can be anguished and self-questioning at times, but when he is out in the landscape, he is looking, touching, tasting, hearing, recording and sketching his observations. He says spring, the season of awakening, exhorts us to be with nature with our whole feeling selves. Like a bell the season rings us out of the sluggishness of winter. Even the lowly weeds have their part to play. Clustered in wheels, they sprout up everywhere, shooting long and lovely and lush. We are invited to caress with the tongue the three 'l' consonants and broad vowels, and let the vibrating sounds of the thrush pierce the ear. These sounds rinse the mind of winter residue, purify us and free us to participate in the growth that is everywhere. We may actually feel in the body the stretching, the actual push and pull of spring. Although the season can be harsh, it is also consoling. Here the poet draws on his favourite colour, blue, to suggest that the heavens are opening their light to us after the darkness of winter. All nature knows this and the racing lambs tell us something new is happening.

As usual, in the reflective sestet, Hopkins asks what are we invited into with all this beauty and what are we bidden to do? What, asks the poet, with his musical ear, is this 'strain' I can hear in the universe? Ever the theological poet, he answers: it is the grace of our original creation which calls to us not to forget who we are. In his Scotistic universe, all was given to us in the beginning, since from the beginning God created all things in Christ. Sadly, we forget. Our vision is dulled, our will is weakened and we 'sour with sinning'. It is true that we are still blessed by moments when we glimpse the purity of this original grace as in the eyes of children, but the poet who knows human nature says we need help. As Hopkins can be about what he considers important as a priest, he calls on, even commands Christ – the 'maid's child' and true inscape of the original creation, who said the divine kingdom belongs to little children (Mt 19:14) – to set about this task as saviour, to 'get' in us what is still unspoilt, what we glimpse in the innocence of children, and restore us to 'the sweet being' of our beginnings.

Spring

Nothing is so beautiful as Spring—
  When weeds, in wheels, shoot long and lovely and lush;
  Thrush's eggs look little low heavens, and thrush
Through the echoing timber does so rinse and wring
The ear, it strikes like lightnings to hear him sing;
  The glassy peartree leaves and blooms, they brush
  The descending blue; that blue is all in a rush
With richness; the racing lambs too have fair their fling.

What is all this juice and all this joy?
  A strain of the earth's sweet being in the beginning
In Eden garden.—Have, get, before it cloy,

  Before it cloud, Christ, lord, and sour with sinning,
Innocent mind and Mayday in girl and boy,
  Most, O maid's child, thy choice and worthy the winning.

Gulls at Rosses Point, Sligo, 1933

The Sea and the Skylark

THIS IS another sonnet from Hopkins's Welsh days, his 'salad days', written in April and May 1877. It arises from a 'hearing' experience he had at Rhyl in North Wales, on the Irish Sea. Rhyl was (and still is) a holiday resort, especially during the summer months, and Hopkins often took a break there. In the late nineteenth century it was becoming 'a shallow and frail town', a ghost town in the non-holiday season, developing rootless suburbs and accommodating itself to the incursions of the mining industry.

Backing out from Admiralty Pier, Holyhead, Anglesey, Wales, 1926

Two natural sounds for 'ear and ear', as old and fresh and unspoilt as nature itself, come to Hopkins from opposite directions as he walks by the sea in a westerly direction. It may be late evening or night, since he refers to the moon's influence on the tides. The noises 'trench'– penetrate – his senses, varying from the 'low lull-off' of the sea to its 'roar'. To his left, the lark is singing his heart out as he ascends almost vertically upwards. The poet imagines the lark singing from a musical score and that its instrument is a winch with a spool, ribbon and bobbin of silk, which unwind as the lark moves into the air. We note the vowelling upwards of the language to convey the ascent, and how the lark pours and pelts music, as it 'deals out that being indoors each one dwells'('As Kingfishhers Catch Fire'). As in 'Spring', the noises in their purity 'rinse and wring the ear', and are heard by him as 'strain of earth's sweet being in the beginning.'

The sestet or 'turn' of the sonnet is unusually pessimistic for Hopkins. Critics have said that he has little sympathy for common human emotions and the common man's needs for progress. Be that as it may, readers today who are more in tune with ecological concerns will find in the poet an incipient awareness of care for the earth for the earth's sake which is also a care for our own human good. In the last lines he addresses both these truths theologically though obscurely. He takes issue with a Darwinian view of scientific naturalism, the human arising from the slime of earth and the human somehow being determined by it. He opts for the biblical view of Genesis, and of a creative divine design for the universe. In this view also human beings, the 'cheer and charm' and crown of creation have responsibility to bring the earth to the goal the Creator intends for it. But when we over-identify with the progress of 'our make and making', we renounce even our deepest selves as image of God. With stark, even harsh words, he warns of the possible degeneration of the human and the environment as everything is reduced to the godless pre-creation slime that was the nothingness of the universe before the divine creative act.

The Sea and the Skylark

On ear and ear two noises too old to end
Trench—right, the tide that ramps against the shore;
With a flood or a fall, low lull-off or all roar,
Frequenting there while moon shall wear and wend.

Left hand, off land, I hear the lark ascend,
His rash-fresh re-winded new-skeinèd score
In crisps of curl off wild winch whirl, and pour
And pelt music, till none 's to spill nor spend.

How these two shame this shallow and frail town!
How ring right out our sordid turbid time,
Being pure! We, life's pride and cared-for crown,

Have lost that cheer and charm of earth's past prime:
Our make and making break, are breaking, down
To man's last dust, drain fast towards man's first slime.

Hurrahing in Harvest

In a letter to Robert Bridges, Hopkins says that this sonnet is the outcome of half an hour of extreme enthusiasm as he walked home alone one day from fishing in the Elwy River.[17] The poem is dated 1 September 1877. While it is a very joyous poem, there is also a sadness. Not invited back for another year of theology, Hopkins is saying goodbye to his beloved Wales and to the Clwyd valley on which he looked down from the height of St Beuno's. The Vale of Clwyd is a basin surrounded by hills, with mighty Snowdon to the west. Hopkins would have walked home that day through the valley. There is an exhilarating joyousness and movement in this poem and it is conveyed by the rhythm. Read aloud, we note the movement of sprung rhythm, and we find ourselves tripping along naturally with the words like a deer watching its step as it comes down a mountainside.

There are staccato moments which claim our attention: 'Summer ends now', with the stress on 'ends'; and 'I walk, I lift up, I lift up heart, eyes', where the stress is on deliberate actions of the poet, as if they are being done for the last time. And then there is such a variety of colour. Above all, one is hit by yellowness and the 'barbarous', elemental beauty of the cornfields. MacKenzie suggests that 'the unkempt stooks are like 'grass-skirted tribesmen'[18] – hence the pagan energy of the poem. Overhead is the moving world of clouds. We note here the chiming of consonants and how the 'meal-drift' clouds reflect the colour of the cornfields. When Hopkins looks up, he wants to stay up there and he asks the reader to join him.

MacKenzie tells us that the poet's leap of imagination was also suggested by the landscape. In the rich mistiness of autumn, the hills can seem hung with blue, cut off from the fields below, and heaved up into the air as though by a giant or divine Colossus.[19] And so we must raise ourselves up with the poet to walk the 'wind-walks' among the clouds and from there look 'Down all that glory in the heavens'. The effect

'Barbarous in beauty, the stooks rise', wrote Hopkins. And what he called 'silk-sack clouds' were photographed by Father Browne in County Laois, 1938

of beauty on the poet as always is to call on God, to give beauty back to 'beauty's self and beauty's giver'(in 'The Leaden Echo, The Golden Echo'). Now, in the cornfield, he says he must consciously 'glean our Saviour', who he feels is giving himself to him on this day with such real, round and rapturous replies. What is more real, he imagines, than being up there in the 'wind-walks' amid the clouds, 'accompanying the Saviour, who, like a mighty stallion, 'stalwart', and having the sweetness of divine energy, bears the world on his azurous shoulders. It is possible here that Hopkins may be influenced by Psalm 19:1–6. Christian biblical commentary on the psalm would see Christ, the Sun of Justice, as Risen Lord coming like a bridegroom from his chamber, like an Atlantean giant, a champion to run his course. As in stanza 33 of 'The Wreck of the Deutschland', we also meet Christ, 'the passion-plunged giant risen' in the storm of the limitless strides he takes to bring salvation.

A feeling of regret is expressed in the last lines, however. He says it's all there for us, 'but the beholder / Wanting'. He does not indulge the emotion, but, returning again to the original rapture of the experience, he raises himself with the wings of the heart. Momentarily, he hurls off the distractions of earth for the Saviour, although it's a half hurling off of earthiness and preoccupations, for the incarnate Lord is no vague airy presence, but is also present in the very tangibility of earth itself.

Hopkins was ordained to the priesthood on 23 September 1877. The stability of the St Beuno's period is now broken and he is posted between ministries of teaching and parish duties. He speaks of himself as 'fortune's football' at this time, and says that in certain urban postings his muse turns sullen for months at a time. Yet he continues to write, and his poems tells us much about Hopkins, the man and priest, and about the people he chooses as subjects for his poetry.

Hurrahing in Harvest

Summer ends now; now, barbarous in beauty, the stooks arise
Around; up above, what wind-walks! what lovely behaviour
Of silk-sack clouds! has wilder, wilful-wavier
Meal-drift moulded ever and melted across skies?

I walk, I lift up, I lift up heart, eyes,
Down all that glory in the heavens to glean our Saviour;
And, eyes, heart, what looks, what lips yet gave you a
Rapturous love's greeting of realer, of rounder replies?

And the azurous hung hills are his world-wielding shoulder
Majestic—as a stallion stalwart, very-violet-sweet!—
These things, these things were here and but the beholder
Wanting; which two when they once meet,
The heart rears wings bold and bolder
And hurls for him, O half hurls earth for him off under his feet.

City street with pedestrians, Liverpool, Merseyside, 1939

Part Two

FORTUNE'S FOOTBALL

Oxford, Liverpool, Glasgow, Stonyhurst

Binsey Poplars

felled 1879

In December 1878, Hopkins was transferred to The Oxford Oratory Church of St Aloysius Gonzaga, a Jesuit church on St Giles' Road, Oxford, where he was stationed for ten months. It was during that time that he wrote the wistful 'Binsey Poplars', inscribing 'felled 1879' immediately after the title to emphasise the irreplaceable loss of these particular trees.

Binsey was a village in Oxford. The poplars gave it its beauty, and in destroying them something of Binsey itself was lost. These aspens, like other poplars, stand tall with pipe-like trunks. Here they are ranked in a row by the river bank, their broad leaves like cages quelling 'the leaping sun'. For the poet, they are 'My aspens dear'. He mimics the destruction of their particular inscape with the sonorous repetition of 'felled'. We can hear the fatal blows of the axe. But here the poet recalls his student days, when these airy leafy cages, like schoolgirls, dandled their leafy sandalled shadows over the moving waters.

In the second verse he picks up the heaviness of 'felled' again, with language of delving, hewing, hacking and racking. It is not the language of life, nor of 'the growing green!' It is the language of death and ending, and the poet feels it keenly. We note the desperation in his tone in the second verse. Country inscapes are delicate and tender. Like any organism, what we have come to cherish ecologically today as the great ball of earth can be disfigured as easily as can the human eye by the jab of a needle. Even in good faith, we act out of a blindness, and we deprive future generations of the beauty that has been. Inscapes are 'especial' because they are 'selves'.

Of each inscape, he says in 'As Kingfishers Catch Fire', 'myself it speaks and spells'. They are unrepeatable. Can the poet voice it more strongly that this? There is no suggestion of 'the dearest freshness deep down things' coming to the rescue as in 'God's Grandeur'. We are left with bleakness and loss and they reverberate more deeply in the mind with the repetition in the last lines.

Binsey Poplars

My aspens dear, whose airy cages quelled,
Quelled or quenched in leaves the leaping sun,
All felled, felled, are all felled;
Of a fresh and following folded rank
Not spared, not one
That dandled a sandalled
Shadow that swam or sank
On meadow and river and wind-wandering weed-winding bank.

O if we but knew what we do
When we delve or hew—
Hack and rack the growing green!
Since country is so tender
To touch, her being so slender,
That, like this sleek and seeing ball
But a prick will make no eye at all,
Where we, even where we mean
To mend her we end her,
When we hew or delve:
After-comers cannot guess the beauty been.
Ten or twelve, only ten or twelve
Strokes of havoc únselve
The sweet especial scene,
Rural scene, a rural scene,
Sweet especial rural scene.

'Towery city and branchy between towers': Oxford

Duns Scotus's Oxford

This very fine poem was written in March 1879 while Hopkins was ministering at St Aloysius. Back after eight years, he loves this 'towery city'. The first two verses are in praise of Oxford, although he notes some changes. Yet for the poet something has not changed, that subtle something in the air, that certain atmosphere that is still there, even six hundred years later, since the Franciscan priest and philosopher, Duns Scotus, lived there as a don and taught at Merton College. The last two verses are the poet's paean to his mentor Scotus.

'Branchy between towers' symbolises the harmony between country and city, town and gown that is Oxford. The first line opens us to the tree-lined streets and fields that for centuries blended so beautifully with the grey stone of old Oxford, where nature was balanced against human nature and those 'coped and poised powers' of the intellectual and religious imagination were reconciled, as were the sounds of birds, bells and running waters of the 'river-rounded' city. The jaggedness of the hyphenated words of the second line conveys the noise and busyness of Oxford, but it is an acceptable noise.

In the second verse he bemoans the graceless growth that surrounds the city. Yellow brick buildings are not neighbourly to the grey beauty of this town. He laments the human loss and also the 'keeping' or care that rural communities naturally give to their 'folk, flocks, and flowers'.

But Oxford will always matter to him as a poet because Duns Scotus lived here, breathing the same air, surrounded by the same weeds and waters, his spirit haunting its walls. 'Of realty the rarest-veined unraveller'. Hopkins chooses his words carefully, indeed he coins one, 'realty', to convey in one line the gift of the philosopher known as 'The Subtle Doctor'. As we have seen, the poet had a special kinship with the way Scotus understood the real, because the philosopher held that everything created has its being as a distinctive individual essence, and is not just a clone of an abstract form or essence. Each 'this' and 'that' of the universe, animate and non-animate, cries out its own inscape or self. As we have seen, the philosopher validates the poet's aesthetic, and so Hopkins can say of Scotus that he 'of all men most sways my spirits to peace'.

Hopkins is aware, however, that in the scholastic world, the Subtle Doctor is not widely studied or accepted as mainstream, so he turns to a theological point, where it cannot be denied that in the formulation of the Catholic doctrine on the Immaculate Conception of Mary, Scotus's contribution was crucial. Coming at the end of a poem which is largely about the inscape of Oxford as an ambience of the philosopher, the reference to this Marian doctrine might seen like an intrusion. But the poet wishes to give due credit to his mentor, for in Paris in 1301 Scotus fired all of France (not England, regrettably for the poet!) in disputation with scholars and divines, especially those of great standing who were linked with the tradition of Aquinas (Italy) and the latter's interpretation of Greek philosophy. Scotus simply pointed out that in the area of healing/redemption, prevention is better than cure, that the highest act of Christ's redeeming power was not just to cure sin, but to prevent it in the first place. It was possible for God to prepare a human being worthy to be the mother of his Son, and this is what the Creator did in the Jewish Mary. The doctrine is not in scripture but it had been in the devotion of Christians through the centuries. It is a very Franciscan doctrine, a victory of the affective over neat rational systems. On 8 December 1854, it was defined as a dogma of faith by Pope Pius IX.

Duns Scotus's Oxford

Towery city and branchy between towers;
Cuckoo-echoing, bell-swarmèd, lark-charmèd, rook-racked,
   river-rounded;
The dapple-eared lily below thee; that country and town did
Once encounter in, here coped and poisèd powers;

Thou hast a base and brickish skirt there, sours
That neighbour-nature thy grey beauty is grounded
Best in; graceless growth, thou hast confounded
Rural rural keeping—folk, flocks, and flowers.

Yet ah! this air I gather and I release
He lived on; these weeds and waters, these walls are what
He haunted who of all men most sways my spirits to peace;

Of realty the rarest-veinèd unraveller; a not
Rivalled insight, be rival Italy or Greece;
Who fired France for Mary without spot.

The Handsome Heart

at a Gracious answer

I include this small poem, dated 1879, as a reminder that the range of Hopkins's poetry is wider than nature poems. He also writes about people, especially those given to him in his professional life as a priest. It has been said that friendships were important to the Victorians – in a reading of Hopkins's journals and letters, which are much more numerous than his poems, we find many accounts of his friendships. He was surprised that Robert Bridges liked the poem, because he himself thought it uneven in quality and needing polish. During Holy Week he was under pressure as his parish priest was away recovering from an accident. Two boys from poor families (the Italian father of one was a seller of ices) gave him much help in the sacristy, and he wants to give each a money gift in gratitude. They both refuse. One boy, however, agrees to accept a book that the poet would choose for him. The poem focuses on Hopkins's relationship with this one boy, and it attempts to voice the delicate experience of that relationship, which was for the poet a meeting with the distinctive inscape of the young person.

In the first verse, the boy is 'plied and pressed', but, just as the needle of a compass springs back to its original reading, the boy comes back to his 'first poised purport of reply'. In the second verse, Hopkins, as in 'Spring', is filled with wonder at the nature of an uncorrupted heart, and says that the boy, like a carrier pigeon, is blessed with a homing instinct. So well taught is he that this personal 'fine function' falls lightly and naturally on his young shoulders, 'wild' – a word beloved of the poet and meaning unspoilt – and simply arising from his nature.

The poet's problem now is not what money gift to give the boy but how to help in some way someone already so graced. In the last two verses, the Jesuit priest speaks with a blessing and prayer for the boy, a blessing for his handsome heart and natural wisdom which are more than a handsome face, and prayer, in the spirit of St Paul, that this boy will stay in the race and brace himself to win the wreath that will never wither (1 Cor 9:24–27). It is of interest that in a later letter Hopkins tells Robert Bridges that the hero of the poem had gone to school in Boulogne to further his education with a view to becoming a priest and a Jesuit.[20]

'Wild and self-instressed'. Sand Art, Balbriggan (1948)

The Handsome Heart

at a Gracious Answer

'BUT tell me, child, your choice; what shall I buy
You?'—'Father, what you buy me I like best.'
With the sweetest air that said, still plied and pressed,
He swung to his first poised purport of reply.

What the heart is! which, like carriers let fly—
Doff darkness, homing nature knows the rest—
To its own fine function, wild and self-instressed,
Falls light as ten years long taught how to and why.

Mannerly-hearted! more than handsome face—
Beauty's bearing or muse of mounting vein,
All, in this case, bathed in high hallowing grace...

Of heaven what boon to buy you, boy, or gain
Not granted?—Only ... O on that path you pace
Run all your race, O brace sterner that strain!

Felix Randal

HOPKINS' next assignment, from 29 October 1879, was in Liverpool, a teeming port city with poor Irish working-class families and sprawling slums. But he was to write later that he found the charming cheery heartiness of Lancashire Catholics deeply comforting. He was based in the parish church of St Francis Xavier's, where the Jesuits had the reputation for magnificent preaching before large numbers. It was hoped that Hopkins, with his Oxford education and mastery of rhetoric, would shine there, but what happens in this poem is that the success that accrues to him comes more from a human and pastoral relationship.

Biographers and acquaintances tell of a vulnerability and innocence in the poet's love for people. There was a humility before everyone he met and a fascination with the different and 'other' that is the hallmark of his poetry. In this poem his relationship is with a parishioner, a young blacksmith who is dying of tuberculosis. So many things happen in this lovely poem, and reading it aloud helps to hold them together. In reading aloud we appreciate how the rhythm of the long, rangy, jagged lines mimic the mould of the 'big-boned and hardy handsome' farrier in the grim forge, who, with easy and careless stride, can turn to find his random tools where and when he needs them. Now this man is wasting away in death.

Hopkins imagines how, in the days of his prime, he was powerful amid his peers, being the equal of the great horses he worked with. The magnificent Shires and Clydesdales used for pulling heavy brewers' drays stood nearly six feet high at the shoulders. Only unusual natural strength could cope with the blacksmith's trade.

We find Hopkins identifies with the farrier both as poet and priest. We note the sensitivity of his inclusion of the Lancashire dialect – 'all road ever he offended'. All is now forgiven by the sacrament, and the fear of death is assuaged. And it is touching, though not cloying, how the poet as priest, with words like 'endear', 'tears' and 'touch', appreciates how the dying man affirms him in his priestly ministry and makes him feel he has something to give.

Paul Mariani suggests in his commentary that 'shield' is the underthought or inscape of this poem. Both farrier and poet act as what in God's eye they are, shields, the priest providing a shield for the farrier in face of death, and the farrier providing shields from the streets and roads for the great drayhorses.[21] Incidentally, the farrier, a parishioner who died at the age of thirty-one, was Felix Spenser, not Felix Randal. Either Hopkins's gentlemanly Victorian decorum would not allow him to use a contemporary's name in a creative work, or he wanted a name with symbolic resonance. ('Randal' of Anglo-Saxon origin, means a 'shield', a strip of leather placed on the heel of a shoe to protect it.) The poet, however, retains the farrier's personal name, Felix, which means 'happy', because it links Felix's spirit of his 'more boisterous years' when he went about his work with rough good humour, with the spirit of his 'heavenlier heart' in the final journey.

The intensity and nobility Hopkins attributes to the man's everyday work is sourced in the poet's priestly vision that no work is trivial in the light of the Incarnation. As he wrote in 'As Kingfishers Catch Fire', 'Christ plays' in all our works. However, Hopkins is a poet, and his poetic concerns are never far from the surface. In the unforgettable final two lines, he seems to see himself in the blacksmith, and, indeed, can identify with the ambience of the 'grim forge' as a place of creativity. He, too, makes his poems at a great cost to himself. He, too, fettles them on the anvil and they come red hot from his experience of beauty, which is indistinguishable from his mastery of words. These words he chooses carefully and pounds them to make them shine and ring out their pure music.

As Seamus Heaney said, Hopkins is 'a poet of fire and flint, not of marsh-light'.[22] He has left us some unforgettable 'bright and battering' 'sandals', with a refreshing elemental quality of which we never tire.

Smithy at work, Lisnaskea, Fermanagh, 1930

Felix Randal

Felix Randal the farrier, O he is dead then? my duty all ended,
Who have watched his mould of man, big-boned and hardy-handsome
Pining, pining, till time when reason rambled in it and some
Fatal four disorders, fleshed there, all contended?

Sickness broke him. Impatient he cursed at first, but mended
Being anointed and all; though a heavenlier heart began some
Months earlier, since I had our sweet reprieve and ransom
Tendered to him. Ah well, God rest him all road ever he offended!

This seeing the sick endears them to us, us too it endears.
My tongue had taught thee comfort, touch had quenched thy tears,
Thy tears that touched my heart, child, Felix, poor Felix Randal;

How far from then forethought of, all thy more boisterous years,
When thou at the random grim forge, powerful amidst peers,
Didst fettle for the great grey drayhorse his bright and battering sandal!

Spring and Fall

to a young child

THERE IS something exquisitely right about this poem. Hopkins composed it on 7 September 1880, while walking back from one of his Liverpool duties of saying Mass in the country house of a Catholic family in Lydiate, outside the city. It seems quite a spontaneous composition. Unusual for the poet, the poem is not about a particular incident or place or person.

Margaret is a little girl of his imagination and Goldengrove is a metaphor with romantic associations of living in a golden or forever time. Written in couplets, it is directed to the child, the language simple and moving like a musical piece. (Hopkins had, in fact, composed some music to accompany it, but it was lost.) Yet there is tension here. It is already present in the title, in the juxtaposition of the opposites, 'Spring and Fall'. The poet does not address this tension abstractly but plays it out through Margaret's feelings as a child and, later, as an adult.

The poet marvels at the child's grieving for the falling of leaves and addresses her with the warning that, 'as the heart grows older it will come to such sights colder'. The pace of the poem gathers speed here with the change from couplets to a triplet, which expresses the nub, and the lyric then subsides into three final couplets. The nub of the poem seems to be that the older Margaret, with her clearer mind, will know that what she mourns for as a child is not the falling of leaves, nor the fact that whole forests are becoming 'wanwood' (colourless), or that billions of leaves are becoming meal for the earth, but rather her own 'falling', her death. Again, to Margaret the child he says, to name this for you at this moment does not matter, but the springs of all sorrow are the same, and this you will come to know in your way through your heart and spirit ('ghost').

The word 'Fall' broods over the whole poem, and its other meaning of original sinfulness is conveyed as 'the blight man was born for'. With the use of 'for' rather than 'with', Hopkins implies that we must face up to the human condition. He does

Young girl, Tubbercurry, Co. Sligo, 1933

not indulge this doctrine further, nor does he ease it, as we might expect, with the truth of redemption in Christ. Rather, he leaves us with the naked and salutary realism of a 'suffered world' of which we are part. Because of the Fall (implicit in the poem's title) a thousand springs of sorrow spring up from this one great underground stream.

The poet had first-hand experience of some of these springs. There was his poor health, and, as he confided to a friend, he found 'Liverpool of all places the most museless. It is indeed a most unhappy and miserable spot.'[23]

Spring and Fall

to a young child

Margaret, are you grieving
Over Goldengrove unleaving?
Leaves, like the things of man, you
With your fresh thoughts care for, can you?
Ah! as the heart grows older
It will come to such sights colder
By and by, nor spare a sigh
Though worlds of wanwood leafmeal lie;
And yet you will weep and know why.
Now no matter, child, the name:
Sorrow's springs are the same.
Nor mouth had, no nor mind, expressed
What heart heard of, ghost guessed:
It is the blight man was born for,
It is Margaret you mourn for.

Inversnaid

THROUGHOUT July and August 1881, Hopkins had his Liverpool rounds of Masses, hearing confessions, visiting the sick and those in the workhouse, serving as chaplain to various Catholic organisations and setting up poor boxes for their relief. He even tried to get annulments for failed marriages. No poetry came to him, just musical composition when he had access to a piano. However, referring back to that time in which he wrote 'Binsey Poplars', some other lines were found among his notes: 'O where is it, the wilderness, / The wildness of the wilderness? / Where is it, the wilderness? … / And wander in the wilderness; / In the weedy wilderness, / Wander in the wilderness'.[24]

The wildness of the wilderness was given him in a posting to Glasgow, in which he filled in at St Joseph's Church. From there he had a short holiday to Loch Lomond. Exploring the small settlement of Inverness in the Scottish Highlands, his heart opened to the 'lightsome fawn froth of the beadbonny stream' trundling down to the dark waters below. The little river was Arklet Burn, flowing from Loch Arklet in the Trossachs near Loch Lomond. But this is no lightsome Tennysonian brook sparkling its pleasant way through villages under man-made bridges. This Scottish burn is a darksome stream (the Old English 'brun' also implies 'brown') from the peat-brown waters of Loch Arklet. It gleams against the rocks like the groomed brown flanks of a wild young horse whose hooves reverberate on its descent over the stones and boulders. Like the horse, the brook is male. Its cooped-up waters break out with a ribbed effect, giving it a fleecy mane of foam, which narrows to a high spray and then falls to the lake below.

In stanza 2 the fleecy mane, tossed like a 'wind-puffed bonnet', turns and divides in two ('twindles') over the dark broth of the pool. ('Twindles' is not in the standard dictionaries of the time, but it existed in Lancashire dialect, and was used as a noun for

Croft on moor, Kilchomain, Islay, Scotland, 1928

twins.[25]) We get the feeling here that the noisy sparkling burn does not want to enter the 'pitchblack' pool. It stays on the surface, eddying 'rounds and rounds'. Hopkins has another possible meaning for 'rounds' here from the old English 'runian', which means 'whispers'. And he envisages the daring burn in a whispering voice telling black Despair, with its capital D, to go drown itself! It is what the poet also needs to say to Despair in his own life also. He lifts his eyes to survey the luscious landscape around, and how it is irrigated, moist and 'degged' (Lancashire dialect, meaning 'sprinkled') with dew in its 'groins' (depressions made in its banks by the surging water). And all adorned with wiry clumps of Scottish heather, tufts of fern and the knobbly clusters of overhanging red mountain ash.

As always with Hopkins we ask what must we do with such beauty? What does he 'bid' us do in this picturesque and musical poem? Having tasted with him the wildness and wetness and how we need the wilderness to enlarge and heal our own human selving, he makes one plea to us: 'Let them be left'. The repetition in the lines has the force of a prayer.

Inversnaid

This darksome burn, horseback brown,
His rollrock highroad roaring down,
In coop and in comb the fleece of his foam
Flutes and low to the lake falls home.

A windpuff-bonnet of fawn-froth
Turns and twindles over the broth
Of a pool so pitchblack, fell-frowning,
It rounds and rounds Despair to drowning.

Degged with dew, dappled with dew
Are the groins of the braes that the brook treads through,
Wiry heathpacks, flitches of fern,
And the beadbonny ash that sits over the burn.

What would the world be, once bereft
Of wet and of wildness? Let them be left,
O let them be left, wildness and wet;
Long live the weeds and the wilderness yet.

Ribblesdale

IN SEPTEMBER 1882, Hopkins was given the option of going to Stonyhurst College to teach Classics and English literature to students preparing for university. Viewing the noble Lancashire countryside from the college's acres of flat roof he leaves us with a stunning description of 'Pendle Hill, Ribblesdale, the fells, and all around, bleakish but solemn and beautiful'.[26] At Stoneyhurst he began his first sonnet after two years. 'Ribblesdale' is a companion-piece to an earlier Welsh sonnet, 'The Valley of the Elwy', in which Hopkins had presented a picture of nature where only man did not fit:

> Lovely the woods, waters, meadows, combes, vales,
> All the air things wear that build the world of Wales;
> Only the inmate does not correspond.

It is helpful for the reading of 'Ribblesdale' to include the epigraph from St Paul that prefaced it in the manuscript. It is Romans 8:20, but I set it in context here of the larger reading that must have inspired the poet: 'For the creation waits with eager longing for the revealing of the children of God; for the creation was subjected to futility, not of its own will but by the will of the one who subjected it, in hope that the creation itself will be set free from its bondage and will attain the freedom of the glory of the children of God' (Rom 8:19–21).

Hopkins is aware of the pathos of landscape. He capitalises Earth in lines 1 and 9, and Ribblesdale and its river are the voice of inarticulate nature as a whole. Already a dissonance appears in the first stanza, with throng and 'louched low' (bent down) suggesting overcrowding and slouching in the way crowds in Liverpool and Glasgow can press upon pedestrians in the street. Nature here is becoming overwhelmed. And nature makes no pleas; it has no heart to feel; it just *is* – and it continues in such a way, 'long', or for ever. Hopkins makes much of this, that nature's gift is just to be itself, and it does this so well, as he tells us in 'As Kingfishers Catch Fire'. Now,

Front of Stoneyhurst taken from the fish pond. Lancashire, England, New Year's Day, 1926

however, we are no longer allowing it to be itself. We do the 'lovely dale down'; we change the course of its rivers. We give everything over 'to rack or wrong'. We, who, in the sestet, he says are 'the eye, tongue' and 'heart' of creation. He does not devalue the human being, for we are 'dear' to each other and the Creator, and also dearly bought by Christ. But Hopkins is realistic. We humans, are dear but 'dogged'. We follow our 'own selfbent' with sullen obstinacy. We wastefully, with no thought for the future, plunder 'our rich round world bare'.

Personifying earth in the last line, he says it is due to our bidding that earth wears 'brows of such care' and shows signs of neglect. This is an unforgiving poem. No tender references to a 'dearest freshness deep down things', nor the brooding presence of the Holy Spirit as in 'God's Grandeur'. There is a moral expectation here. At the end of the nineteenth century, Hopkins is already voicing what Pope Francis will write in *Laudato Sì*, more than a hundred years later. In relation to our common home, the pope writes: 'Our goal is not to amass information or to satisfy curiosity, but rather to become painfully aware, to dare to turn what is happening in the world into our own personal suffering and thus discover what each of us can do about it' (*LS* 19).

Ribblesdale

Earth, sweet Earth, sweet landscape, with leaves throng
And louched low grass, heaven that dost appeal
To, with no tongue to plead, no heart to feel;
That canst but only be, but dost that long—

Thou canst but be, but that thou well dost; strong
Thy plea with him who dealt, nay does now deal,
Thy lovely dale down thus and thus bids reel
Thy river, and o'er gives all to rack or wrong.

And what is Earth's eye, tongue, or heart else, where
Else, but in dear and dogged man?—Ah, the heir
To his own selfbent so bound, so tied to his turn,

To thriftless reave both our rich round world bare
And none reck of world after, this bids wear
Earth brows of such care, care and dear concern.

The Blessed Virgin compared to the Air we Breathe

MAY IS Mary's month. In contributing to a Jesuit custom at Stonyhurst that poems be composed and hung up in praise of Mary, Hopkins wrote this fine Marian poem. Possibly because it was written to order it was not his favourite, and he felt that composition on the highest subjects have to compromise with popular taste. But his reader poets loved the spontaneity and the ease with which it could be read, and even Robert Bridges, his agnostic Anglican friend, appreciated it despite its theme.[27] But this is a memorable poem because Hopkins is so original in his choice of the 'wild air' metaphor, and in the way in which he is in full control of the metaphor right through. He loves wildness. In wildness he feels in touch with the pure 'selving' of things, whether it is the wildness of nature as in 'Inversnaid', the 'wild and self-instressed' heart of the young boy in 'The Handsome Heart'. He chooses the pure wildness of air to express the selving of Mary. Incidentally, air, which is Mary's colour, is also blue. He calls on verbs like nestling, girdling, riddling or interpenetrating to convey that air is the nursing element of the universe. We could exist without food for a while, but never without air. And so, he says, air reminds him – 'Minds me in so many ways' – of Mary, who not only became the mother of God's Son, but also in us is mother 'of each new grace / That does now reach our race'. Recalling the Catholic doctrine of the Immaculate Conception, he says that Mary, merely a woman, is, by God's special grace, untouched by sin, because she has but one work to do: 'Let all God's glory through'.

Hopkins goes further to fill out the selving or inscape of Mary. He says she is the mother of mercy, for we human beings of this 'guilty globe' need her to bring our prayers to God. And we need her even more deeply in her high motherhood, because from that high place of grace, she is enabled to have a part in assuaging the 'deathdance', the propensity to evil in us. The poet here is alluding to the belief, common at least from St Bernard's time, that Christ has chosen to send his gifts to us through Mary as Mediatrix of all Graces. Not wishing to go to extremes in his devotion, he safeguards himself with the reminder that Christ is our Saviour still. But this is a poetry of energy, light and praise, and he does not wish to rein himself in. Mary is inseparable from her Son, and within the 'wild web' of her air, Christ continues to incarnate himself again and again in the universe. Each of us can rise to our destined level of humanity, becoming 'New self and nobler me'. While the poet believes that each of us realises our true selving only in relation to God's redeeming action in us through Christ, he nevertheless asserts the additional Catholic view that our relationship to Christ becomes more tangible and accessible through the mediation of Mary.

To further press this truth, Hopkins resorts to a simple poetic science. He asks us to imagine that if the azured air around us creating the blue sky did not exist, there would be no protection between us and the blear and blinding ball of the sun. The poet's opinion that the God of the Old Testament was dazzling and fearsome comes from a time when there was an absolute divide between Christians and Jews. Biblical studies and Christian-Jewish relations today have bridged that gap. Yet seeing the Old Testament God as Hopkins does makes a case for his argument that we human beings need God to reveal himself to us in a way more amenable to our condition. This is what he did when his Son became one of us in the flesh, and this is what he did with the participation of Mary in that she is the woman who gave a human body to God's Son, making 'our daystar [2 Pet 1:19] / 'Much dearer to mankind'.

The poem ends with a beautiful prayer. Returning again to the metaphor of air and atmosphere, he asks Mary to front his 'froward' or perverse eye. Whenever he is overwhelmed or beyond himself, whether with beauty or the stress of life, we find him praying for the basic virtues of patience, penance and prayer (as in 'The Starlight Night') as a kind of grounding exercise. Indeed, in the last lines, like a son to a mother, he turns to Mary for the happiness that seems to elude him. Although not yet forty, before the writing of this Mary poem, Hopkins's letters to Bridges have spoken of always feeling jaded, and he wrote to Canon Dixon, that he saw 'no grounded prospect for ever doing much not only in poetry but in anything at all'.[28] Yet, when he moves from Stonyhurst to Dublin, and becomes more isolated, from the friends he knew, from family and countrymen, his muse coaxes him to write again, and this time, writing from greater darkness, he confronts God and the self within and leaves us some powerful poems.

The Blessed Virgin compared to the Air we Breathe

Wild air, world-mothering air,
Nestling me everywhere,
That each eyelash or hair
Girdles; goes home betwixt
The fleeciest, frailest-flixed
Snowflake; that 's fairly mixed
With, riddles, and is rife
In every least thing's life;
This needful, never spent,
And nursing element;
My more than meat and drink,
My meal at every wink;
This air, which, by life's law,
My lung must draw and draw
Now but to breathe its praise,
Minds me in many ways
Of her who not only
Gave God's infinity
Dwindled to infancy
Welcome in womb and breast,
Birth, milk, and all the rest
But mothers each new grace
That does now reach our race—
Mary Immaculate,
Merely a woman, yet
Whose presence, power is
Great as no goddess's
Was deemèd, dreamèd; who
This one work has to do—
Let all God's glory through,
God's glory which would go
Through her and from her flow
Off, and no way but so.

I say that we are wound
With mercy round and round
As if with air: the same
Is Mary, more by name.
She, wild web, wondrous robe,
Mantles the guilty globe,
Since God has let dispense
Her prayers his providence:
Nay, more than almoner,
The sweet alms' self is her
And men are meant to share
Her life as life does air.

If I have understood,
She holds high motherhood
Towards all our ghostly good
And plays in grace her part
About man's beating heart,
Laying, like air's fine flood,
The deathdance in his blood;
Yet no part but what will
Be Christ our Saviour still.
Of her flesh he took flesh:5
He does take fresh and fresh,
Though much the mystery how,
Not flesh but spirit now

And makes, O marvellous!
New Nazareths in us,
Where she shall yet conceive
Him, morning, noon, and eve;
New Bethlems, and he born
There, evening, noon, and morn—
Bethlem or Nazareth,
Men here may draw like breath
More Christ and baffle death;
Who, born so, comes to be
New self and nobler me
In each one and each one
More makes, when all is done,
Both God's and Mary's Son.

Again, look overhead
How air is azurèd;
O how! nay do but stand
Where you can lift your hand
Skywards: rich, rich it laps
Round the four fingergaps.
Yet such a sapphire-shot,
Charged, steepèd sky will not
Stain light. Yea, mark you this:
It does no prejudice.
The glass-blue days are those
When every colour glows,
Each shape and shadow shows.
Blue be it: this blue heaven
The seven or seven times seven
Hued sunbeam will transmit
Perfect, not alter it.
Or if there does some soft,
On things aloof, aloft,
Bloom breathe, that one breath more
Earth is the fairer for.
Whereas did air not make
This bath of blue and slake
His fire, the sun would shake,
A blear and blinding ball
With blackness bound, and all
The thick stars round him roll
Flashing like flecks of coal,
Quartz-fret, or sparks of salt,
In grimy vasty vault.

So God was god of old:
A mother came to mould
Those limbs like ours which are
What must make our daystar
Much dearer to mankind;
Whose glory bare would blind
Or less would win man's mind.
Through her we may see him
Made sweeter, not made dim,
And her hand leaves his light
Sifted to suit our sight.

Be thou then, O thou dear
Mother, my atmosphere;
My happier world, wherein
To wend and meet no sin;
Above me, round me lie
Fronting my froward eye
With sweet and scarless sky;
Stir in my ears, speak there
Of God's love, O live air,
Of patience, penance, prayer:
World-mothering air, air wild,
Wound with thee, in thee isled,
Fold home, fast fold thy child.

Newman House, Dublin, where Hopkins lived while in Dublin, and where he died.

Part Three

THE TIMES ARE NIGHTFALL

The Dark Sonnets and other poems

Dublin

The Dark Sonnets: Dublin

On Monday, 18 February 1884, Gerard Manley Hopkins arrived at the Jesuit residence in St Stephen's Green, Dublin. In informing Robert Bridges of his new appointment as Professor of Classics in the new Royal University of Ireland (the revival of John Henry Newman's university, now in the hands of the capable and ebullient John Delany SJ), he made the laconic comment – 'there has been an Irish row over my election.'[29] Hopkins's use of 'Irish' here hints at the complexity of the row, but basically it was about the staffing of the new college. Delany wanted his staff to be on a par with those of Trinity College Dublin and Queen's University Belfast and he looked outside Ireland to the English Jesuit Provincial for help. This caused a rift between him and Archbishop Walsh of Dublin, who felt that a predominance of English scholars was one of the reasons for the failure of Newman's university. Hopkins came reluctantly into this hotbed of nationalism and anti-Britishness. But he had the good will of the English provincial, Fr Pubrick, who may have been relieved that at last one of his men was more suitably placed. But his correspondence with Fr Delany made the demur that this excellent scholar was also eccentric in his ways.[30]

Dublin, one of Britain's greatest cities after London, was a disappointment to the poet. A constant scattering of children of the unemployed erupted from the Liberties onto the streets around St Stephen's Green, begging for pennies and scraps of food. A number of the Anglo-Irish professional class had vacated their homes to move south, away from the stench of the River Liffey which served as the main sewer line for the city. Some of their former homes had been turned into tenements where more than one family lived in a room. But Dublin was no worse than Liverpool or Glasgow. 'My Liverpool and Glasgow experience laid upon my mind a conviction, a truly crushing conviction, of the misery of town life to the poor, of the misery of the poor in general, of the degradation even of our race, of the hollowness of this century's civilisation: it made even life a daily burden to me to have thrust upon me the things I saw.'[31]

The political situation in Ireland was also a source of distress. He writes to his mother of 'the grief of mind I go through over politics'; 'What I read and hear and see in Ireland about Ireland and about England, is such that I can neither express it not bear to speak of it'.[32] Basically conservative and pro empire, he worried about the empire's possible fragmentation under Gladstone and did not favour the repeal of the Act of Union. However, attentive always to suffering of any kind, he did not deny that Ireland was neglected and mismanaged by Britain. Writing of these concerns to his mentor, Blessed J. H. Newman, the latter's pointed reply must have rocked the poet: 'If I were an Irishman, I should be [in heart] a rebel'.[33] Now in Dublin, at least he had the vantage point to make his own assessment.

There were also, however, his lighter side and more playful moments. A gifted mimic with an ear for language, its tone and uses, he was known to have entertained the brethren with a regaling of events in the Hiberno-Irish accent!

Much more could be said about Hopkins's Dublin story, but this book is about the poems. A marvellous first line of one of his Fragments, found among his papers of 1884–5: 'The times are nightfall, look, their light grows less', suggests that he is about to enter the winter period of his life. He admits that what is happening to him must not to be blamed on outside factors. The 'nightfall' is an experience of his own inner self. Lost is his dappled, spring-time world of the earlier Welsh poetry; lost is his family, and lost is Britain, 'the land that bred me'. And yet we find in this inner unravelling of the 'small commonweal' of the self, that his will is in charge and, also, his poetic capacity. He tells us this in the last lines of this Fragment:

> There is your world within.
> There rid the dragons, root out there the sin.
> Your will is law in that small commonweal …

Out of that *commonweal* will come six sonnets, five of which are presented here. They are not easily dated, and they fit in with a few other poems of this Dublin period. They are variously called 'The Terrible Sonnets' (Canon Dixon), 'The Sonnets of Desolation,' (W. H. Gardner) and 'The Dark Sonnets,' (N. H. MacKenzie). 'To Seem the Stranger' is not the first sonnet of this period, but it reads as a preface to the others.

'To seem the stranger'

WRITTEN DURING 1885–6, this sonnet is stark and straightforward in style. A key word is 'stranger', endorsed again at the end of the first line. He finds himself a 'stranger', with his educated upper-class English, in Dublin, which could understand him 'only as an example of English aesthete Catholicism, with which the Irish had no sympathy'.[34]

There is an all-pervading loneliness in the poem, but he handles it methodically, possibly with the hope that by dispassionately looking at what he believes contributes to it, it might evaporate. 'I am at a third / Remove', he says. In fact the 'removes' were there already in his life, but somehow they are now more sharply felt in Ireland. Firstly, there is the separation from his Anglican family due to his conversion and becoming a Jesuit. As Christians, they, too, are 'Brothers and sisters in Christ', but he asks where is Christ now? He who was once his peace seems now his 'parting, sword and strife'. Secondly, there is England, for whom he has a patriot's love, the land of Anglo-Saxon literature and Shakespeare, wife to his creativity, and it does not hear him. The poet is possibly referring here to the rejection of the two shipwreck poems, 'The Wreck of the Deutschland' and 'The Loss of the Eurydice', both considered too odd for publication by the Jesuit cultural journal, *The Month*.

A line deploring the idleness of his creative ability in a perplexing country, so energised by war, introduces the third 'remove' – the personal darkness of spirit that afflicts him. It is accepted that Hopkins suffered from depression during the Dublin years. It is also true that the kind of work he did at the university may also have contributed. As a member of the faculty he taught some Latin and Greek, but his main work as a member of the Royal University was to set and grade exam papers, six times each year, for the BA in Classics for students from all over Ireland. We have his wry comment on this main assignment: 'I examine the nation!' It was tedious work for a person of his temperament, all the more so because of the scrupulous care he brought to it. But there were new relationships in his life and he had his moments of release in visits with Anglo-Catholic friends of his own kind. The sestet concludes

St Stephen's Green in the fog, 1944

with the question once again that most concerns him – blockage in creative work. The listing of factors in his 'remove' does not provide the answer. Am I under some ban from heaven, he wonders, or even under the power of Satan? Must I hoard my writings just for myself and a few friends, and if I do publish, who will understand me? *A Lonely began* in relation to literary colleagues, with whom he hoped for some acceptance. It's as if the times were not ready for the poet who would become a seminal influence in English literature in the twentieth and twenty-first centuries.

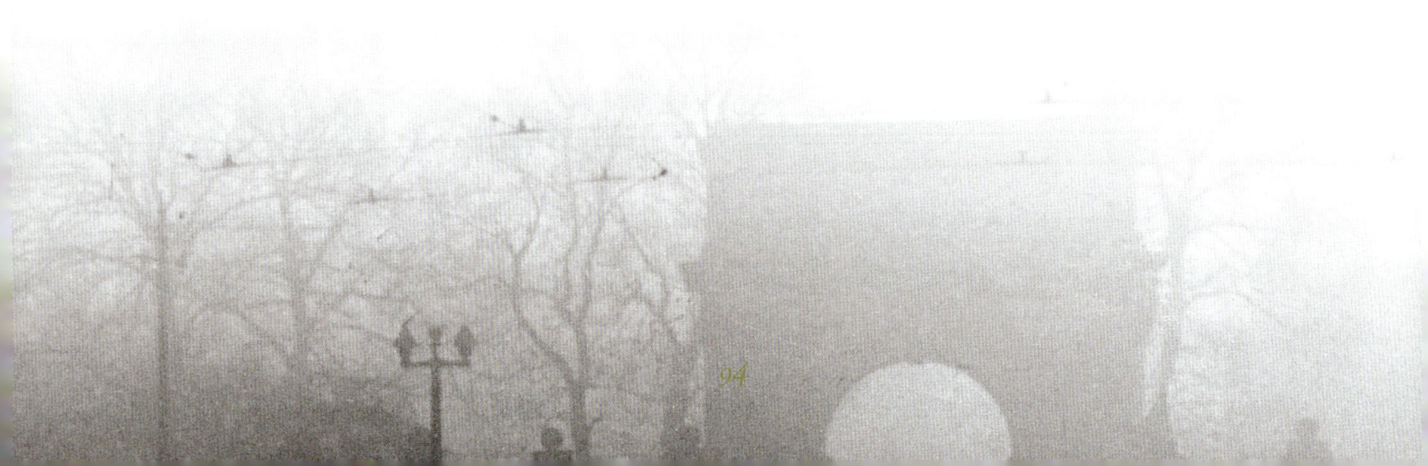

'To seem the stranger'

To seem the stranger lies my lot, my life
Among strangers. Father and mother dear,
Brothers and sisters are in Christ not near
And he my peace my parting, sword and strife.

England, whose honour O all my heart woos, wife
To my creating thought, would neither hear
Me, were I pleading, plead nor do I: I wear-
Y of idle a being but by where wars are rife.

I am in Ireland now; now I am at a third
Remove. Not but in all removes I can
Kind love both give and get. Only what word

Wisest my heart breeds dark heaven's baffling ban
Bars or hell's spell thwarts. This to hoard unheard,
Heard unheeded, leaves me a lonely began.

'I wake and feel'

IN A LATER sonnet, Hopkins speaks of the 'cliffs of fall' of the mind, and warns: 'Hold them cheap / May who ne'er hung there'. Do these words dissuade us from reading these poems? I don't think so. Firstly, Hopkins always remains a poet, no matter the material he works with. Though writing at times of desolation, jadedness and of verging on madness, he implies that his judgement is always intact. Secondly, these sonnets are not emotions recollected in tranquillity; they are direct communications of the poet's feeling at the very moment of composition. As a poet in charge of his material, he always seeks to express its inner design or inscape. In 'As Kingfishers Catch Fire', he addressed the outward 'selves' of birds, stones, bells, human beings, as expressing with their particular 'going' the play of Christ in the universe. Here he attempts to word the inscape of the inner self, now nakedly exposed in desolation. Thirdly, these unruly inner feelings are not thrown out there for us to make of them what we will. They are given rigorous shape with the discipline of the sonnet structure, in which the octave lays out, as it were, the wares, and the sestet is a response or resolution. Indeed, the sonnets are evidence of the poet's holding on to his sanity at this time of his 'winter world'. Fourthly, in the very formality of their structure they have a universality and spaciousness so that they speak for terrified humanity as a whole, and this makes them great poetry. Fifthly, commentators differ as to Hopkins's state of mind in the Dublin years and, indeed, throughout his life, for he was prone to bipolar disorder. But the evidence of his spiritual writings shows that, guided by the Spiritual Exercises of St Ignatius in which he was formed, he interprets these sufferings as God-given, and it is to God he turns in times of both consolation and desolation. While each sonnet stands alone, there is an organic unity between them. 'I Wake and Feel' is the more desolate of the dark sonnets, but as we move through the others we find glimmers of consolation.

The main image of this sonnet's octave is travel, the nightmare image of a man lost in the dark. Hopkins's writings tells us that he always loves light. It enables him to *see* landscapes and vistas, but in this sonnet everything is closed off. Instead of morning light, darkness continues to 'fell' him. The 'fell' experience is like travelling through

Standing at the tip of Malin Head and trying to see Scotland in the distance, 1929

a desolate moor or fell from which there is no rescue; or it can also refer to the hairy hide, or fell, of a large animal who bears down upon him.

In this nightmare darkness the night stretches before him like endless 'black hours' which he fears will envelop his life. All this his heart saw: 'you, heart, saw; ways you went!' It is interesting that in this poem, as in many others, we find numerous references to 'heart'. The heart is 'Mother of being in me', he writes in 'The Wreck of the Deutschland'. Heart is where he is in touch with his true self. But now the cries of his heart go nowhere and remain unheard, like letters sent to a loved dead person.

There are various interpretations of this text. A possible one is that he is reverting to the intense pain he felt as an undergraduate in Oxford when he wrote constant letters to a dear friend, Digby Dolben, and they were unanswered. The live memory is indicative of Hopkins's affections for Dolben, who was later to die in a tragic drowning accident.[35] But it is even more likely that Hopkins is drawing on the power of that memory to help him articulate the desolation he now feels, when God, the one love to whom he has given his life, does not answer his pleas. His use of images of day and night, light and dark, spring from Ignatian teaching. He is aware that Ignatius also counsels on being patient during desolation. The saint's instruction during that time is that God 'may wish to give us a true knowledge and understanding, so that we may truly perceive that it is not within our power to acquire or retain great devotion … or any other spiritual consolation, but that all this is a gift and grace of God our Lord'.[36]

In the sestet he presses on to ask, 'What am I in this darkness without God?' He answers with a piling up of images from the now unlovely human body itself. It is, he says, as if I am under some mysterious divine decree and am thrown on myself alone. And what I find is not pleasant: just the taste of me – only. The old curse wells up here also, the original sinfulness of the 'turned in self'. And while, like yeast, the spirit may enliven the dough of one's being, the poet's response here is sluggish, filled with sour regret and self-loathing. Cut off from God, 'dearest him that lives alas! away', he chooses a powerful phrase to say what this is like. It's like being in the hell of our own 'sweating selves'. Being lost? Yes. Yet, blessedly, not permanently lost. The poem ends with a glimmer of hope. It is very likely that this is the sonnet described by the poet as 'written in blood'.[37]

'I wake and feel'

I wake and feel the fell of dark, not day.
What hours, O what black hoürs we have spent
This night! what sights you, heart, saw; ways you went!
And more must, in yet longer light's delay.

With witness I speak this. But where I say
Hours I mean years, mean life. And my lament
Is cries countless, cries like dead letters sent
To dearest him that lives alas! away.

I am gall, I am heartburn. God's most deep decree
Bitter would have me taste: my taste was me;
Bones built in me, flesh filled, blood brimmed the curse.

Selfyeast of spirit a dull dough sours. I see
The lost are like this, and their scourge to be
As I am mine, their sweating selves; but worse.

'No worst'

THIS POEM circles round the intensity of pain of 'the sweating self' of the previous sonnet and on the limited 'durance' of the poet's own physical frame. He does not call on God here but feels attacked from without by some nameless whirlwind or 'Fury'. His only relief is to call on presences near at hand, the Holy Spirit, the 'Comforter', and 'Mary, mother of us', Consoler of the Afflicted. In the last lines, he falls back on his animal instinct and turns to sleep to end the pain, even as death ends life.

From Dublin, Hopkins once wrote in capital letters to R. Bridges: WHAT DOES ANYTHING MATTER ANYMORE?[58] In this poem, he inscapes an experience something like that, but he also sees it as more than *his* sorrow. It is a 'world-sorrow', which affects us all, a sorrow which winces and sings in us on the 'age-old anvil'. The storm clouds of his cries well up in him with a high pitch or a dull roar. 'Pitch' is a typical Hopkins word. It means the distinctiveness of the self of a thing. In the poet's dappled world everything has its pitch, its irreplaceablility, and nothing in nature comes near the unspeakable stress of pitch of one's own self-being, and that of God, who is infinitely higher in pitch than his creatures.

In the first lines the poet says human beings are naturally pitched or wired to endure suffering, suffering made 'wilder' by the 'forepangs' of past memories. And all this goes on endlessly, and we coalesce together in our cries because we know it is a 'world-sorrow'. He chooses an unexpected rural image here of the heave and huddle of a long herd of animals on a country road. However, if we are momentarily lulled by this image, we are suddenly disrupted by the metallic sound of the anvil, as Fury shrieks: 'No ling- / Ering!' The dividing of the word implies that the time is running out. The poet must move to his assessment, and though he appears to let Fury speak, it is the poet who speaks. 'Let me be fell', he says ('fell' here meaning ruthless, as in 'one fell swoop'), as he introduces the sestet, in which he reaches a resolution that is unsparing of our feelings and his own.

If we are inclined to turn and run, or if you are dismissing all this as histrionics, you are not allowing yourself to be there. In the oft-cited first lines of the sestet he likens the mind, when it is out of its depths, to a mountain climber hanging on the sheer rock face of a cliff, unable to look up or down. (As a young man Hopkins was an avid mountain climber locally, and once went on an expedition to the Swiss Alps.) The image here of being out of one's depth, in a place 'no-man-fathomed', is of the poet being reduced to what he discovers he truly is – 'a Wretch'. And it is from this place that the highly religious, truth-seeking poet knows that he is thrust before the 'no-man-fathomed' God. He can only cry, What is this God saying to me now? But he is a poet, and he is not going to be didactic. He simply hangs in there, taking what animal comfort he can get. 'Here! creep, / Wretch', he says, alluding to Shakespeare's *King Lear*, where the ruined Lear on the cliff in a storm takes refuge in a 'hovel'(Act III Scene 2). Hopkins's hovel is sleep, and even death, if it comes.

'No worst'

No worst, there is none. Pitched past pitch of grief,
More pangs will, schooled at forepangs, wilder wring.
Comforter, where, where is your comforting?
Mary, mother of us, where is your relief?
My cries heave, herds-long; huddle in a main, a chief
Woe, world-sorrow; on an age-old anvil wince and sing—
Then lull, then leave off. Fury had shrieked 'No ling-
ering! Let me be fell: force I must be brief'.
O the mind, mind has mountains; cliffs of fall
Frightful, sheer, no-man-fathomed. Hold them cheap
May who ne'er hung there. Nor does long our small
Durance deal with that steep or deep. Here! creep,
Wretch, under a comfort serves in a whirlwind: all
Life death does end and each day dies with sleep.

Carrion Comfort

THE SONNET was composed in August 1885 while Hopkins was making his annual retreat down the country in Clongowes Wood, County Kildare. He seems to be more in control of his emotions, and, as a whole, the poem reads like a response to the previous two. Death still looms, but a suicidal death is not for the poet: that for him is a corpse-like, 'carrion comfort, a Despair', a giving up. Not for me, he says. Note the repetition of 'not' four times, and the cry of 'I can no more' replaced by 'I can … not choose not to be'.

St Ignatius's counsel is relevant here: 'Let him in desolation labour in patience … and let him think that he soon will be consoled'.[39] Consolation has varying effects. Sometimes it may be a passing sense of the gracious sweetness of God, the memory of which lingers as encouragement; or, as in this sonnet, it is the discovery that God once again is a real presence after so long an absence.

It is also the discovery by the poet that he, too, is real: that he, Gerard Manley Hopkins, while totally dependent on God, freely stands before God, questioning and even wrestling with him. Hopkins reclaims here the biblical attitude of relating to God as in the Psalms. I have always loved the first line of the second stanza of 'The Wreck of the Deutschland', where his colloquy with God begins with – 'I did say yes / O at lightning and lashed rod'.

Only in the last line of this sonnet does the poet use the word 'God'. Throughout the poem it is a divine presence, now become real after a long absence. Hopkins has much to say to this Presence, whom he now confronts as 'O thou terrible'. He turns to the text of Job 10:16: 'Proud as a lion, you hunt me down, multiplying your exploits at my expense, attacking me again and again, your fury upon me ever increasing.' As in Job, Hopkins's God is a lion and the poet bravely fights back, asking, Why do I have to suffer so at your hands? Why, when I was 'heaped there', did you, who wrings the world with your power, rudely 'rock' me, press me further down under your heavy lion limb, turn devouring eyes on me, awesome and passionately loving, and with your tempests fanned me, so that I wanted to flee?

For an additional answer he turns to Christ and to Luke 3:17, where John the Baptist warns that the Messiah who is to come is the Lord of Judgment. With his winnowing fan, Hopkins says he will separate the true grain of my life so it will 'lie sheer and clear'. But in all this time of darkness, the poet remembers that he 'kissed the rod, / Hand rather', kissed the divine will as a merciful hand stretched out to him. And his heart knows that the time has been strangely one of strength, joy and cheer. 'Cheer,' he says cheerily, because the poet is in the 'wring-world' also with the divine being. With Hopkins's fluidity of language, the 'wring-world' of the divine wrestler could also be the *ring*-world of wrestlers. And the poet is right in it.

On the face of it, it is an uneven confrontation between the divine wrestler – Christ, and the poor poet. The questioning language of nervous, short staccato phrases expresses his wonder at the confrontation in that both wrestlers are winners. We are reminded of the beautiful biblical story of Jacob's wrestling with a 'someone' at the Ford of Jabbok (Gen 32:22–32). Jacob is left with a limp but he is a winner in the sense that he gets a blessing from the mysterious stranger. And Hopkins wins in the hope and joy that his now 'done darkness' has abated, at least for a time.

'The Rip' off Melbourne, 1924

Carrion Comfort

Not, I'll not, carrion comfort, Despair, not feast on thee;
Not untwist—slack they may be—these last strands of man
In me or, most weary, cry *I can no more*. I can;
Can something, hope, wish day come, not choose not to be.

But ah, but O thou terrible, why wouldst thou rude on me
Thy wring-world right foot rock? lay a lionlimb against me? scan
With darksome devouring eyes my bruisèd bones? and fan,
O in turns of tempest, me heaped there; me frantic to avoid thee and flee?

Why? That my chaff might fly; my grain lie, sheer and clear.
Nay in all that toil, that coil, since (seems) I kissed the rod,
Hand rather, my heart lo! lapped strength, stole joy, would laugh, cheer.

Cheer whom though? the hero whose heaven-handling flung me, foot trod
Me? or me that fought him? O which one? is it each one? That night, that year
Of now done darkness I wretch lay wrestling with (my God!) my God.

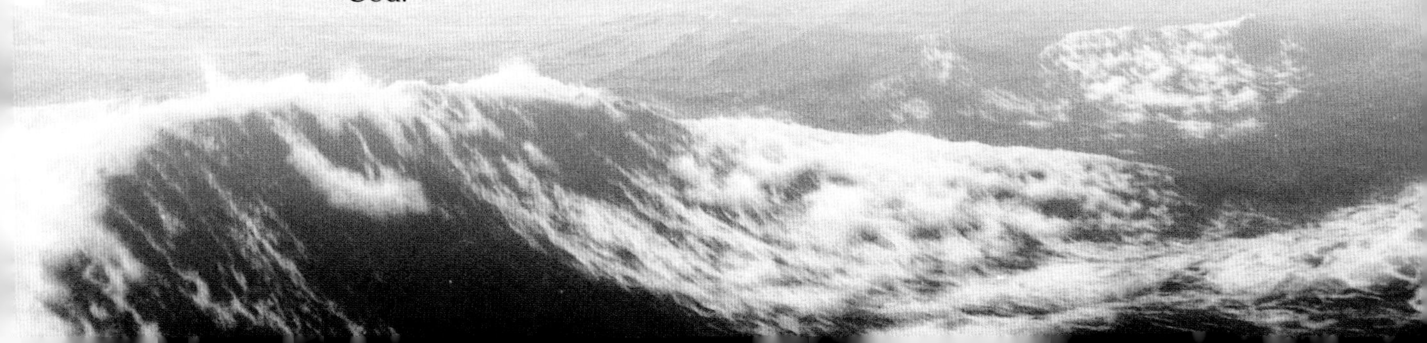

'My own heart'

THIS IS the culmination of the dark sonnets so far, and it is also a heartening poem. In 'Carrion Comfort' Hopkins wrestles for answers from his God, the 'Terrible One'; in this poem he turns with pity to his own heart for wisdom. He is back in Stephen's Green in September after the Clongowes retreat, and in a letter to Robert Bridges he tells of a meeting with a 'hairbrained' friend who asks him to go with him from Kingstown (now Dún Laoghaire) on a yacht for a few days. Hopkins wrote of the outing: 'when I resigned myself to it, I could not help enjoying it.' This was a spontaneous response from the highly controlled Hopkins, and commentator, Paul Mariani, sees it as a lovely mile of smile breaking on the poet's life. He links it with this sonnet, composed around this time.[40] Let me be kind to myself, the poet says. Let me be free of torment: the triple use of different forms of the word express the knots he was tying himself into. He casts (searches) for 'comfort', 'comfort' here having intonations of the Holy Spirit as the Comforter he desperately called upon in 'No Worst There is None'. But he cannot receive comfort because the self to receive it hangs nowhere, like the word 'comfortless' itself, which hangs without a noun in the sentence. It is like a blindness which makes him incapable of seeing, even in the daytime, and it is like a pure thirst he cannot slake in the midst of wet.

In the sestet, he catches himself on – and reprimands himself for still casting around with the bloodhounds of his thoughts. No wonder his poor self, his 'Jackself', dulled by the proverbial 'all work' and no play, is 'jaded'. 'Let be', he says, so that 'comfort' may have more room in you and joy be larger in your life. We are touching on the deep complexity of the poet here. He was an over-wrought personality and quite scrupulous, the latter attributable partly to the fact that he was a convert and brought with him the unbending rectitude of Victorian High Anglicanism.[41]

It is also true that the sestet is guided by the poet's understanding of Ignatian consolation, which God metes out as God wishes in God's own time. And as Hopkins's retreat notes say: the greater the disproportion between what we expect and what is given is a sign that the consolation is from God.[42] So the poem ends on a sublime

Evening shadows, St Stephen's Green, 1939

note with consolation's metaphor as God's 'smile'. Totally gift and unforeseen, it is like an unexpected exposure to the light of large skies as they 'Betweenpie [dapple] mountains', and 'light a lovely mile'.

The ending of the poem hearkens back to the springtime world of Wales and 'Hurrahing in Harvest', in which the giant Christ's shoulder, wedged between the hills, upholds the world. A joyous, straightforward finding God of in nature belonged to that time. But the sonnets of desolation, from the winter world of Dublin, echo Psalm 130, where the poet goes down into the depths of his being and cries out from there to God to hear him.

'My own heart'

My own heart let me have more have pity on; let
Me live to my sad self hereafter kind,
Charitable; not live this tormented mind
With this tormented mind tormenting yet.

I cast for comfort I can no more get
By groping round my comfortless, than blind
Eyes in their dark can day or thirst can find
Thirst 's all-in-all in all a world of wet.

Soul, self; come, poor Jackself, I do advise
You, jaded, let be; call off thoughts awhile
Elsewhere; leave comfort root-room; let joy size

At God knows when to God knows what; whose smile
'S not wrung, see you; unforeseen times rather—as skies
Betweenpie mountains—lights a lovely mile.

To what serves Mortal Beauty?

THIS SONNET was written during a retreat at Clongowes Wood, County Kildare, on 23 August 1885. The topic was an inescapable one for the priest-poet and one he always struggled with: how to reconcile his sensuous love-response to beauty, in all its dapple of nature and human beings, with his primary love, the love of God.

There is a certain didactic clarity about the poem, possibly because he treats the topic as an ethical issue and offers some advice to readers and himself. As a poem of the Hopkins corpus it has not received as much attention as it deserves. Perhaps readers ask if the issue is real, and why does the poet torture himself so? Some critics say that it is a poem that lacks aesthetic appeal. I think that by this they mean that nobody likes to be so clearly presented with the resolution. They like to find it for themselves, as they can do in Hopkins's great poems, which have a capaciousness in which one may wander around, taking from them what one wills, a truth, a pleasure or both. Yet I have always liked this poem because at its centre is a historical gem, which must have entranced Hopkins.

Focusing on the human being, 'World's loveliest', he asks what is the purpose of the beauty that flashes 'off frame and face'? It can excite physical passions and we want to 'seal' it, hold on to it greedily for ourselves, or more creatively as artists desiring to respond to it in a personal way. Indeed, Hopkins does this in many of his poems, such as 'Henry Purcell', which is his response to the unconscious beauty of Purcell's music (Henry Purcell was a seventeenth-century composer and organist at Westminster Abbey). Beauty, says Hopkins, 'keeps warm / Men's wits to the things that are'. Recalling his mentor, John Henry Newman, beauty moves us beyond notional knowledge to realisation; engaging our senses and emotions, it wakes us up. But, he warns, a glance, rather than an intrusive gaze, is enough.

And we do not have to be miserly about beauty. It originates in Divine Beauty and there are no limits to the abundance of its giving. Hopkins recalls an incident from the Venerable Bede's *Ecclesiastical History of England's Conversion to Christianity*, where Pope Gregory the Great, walking through a crowded Roman market, noticed

A young woman fixes her hair using a mirror propped on a rock. Achill Island, Co. Mayo (1939).

some recently arrived fair-haired and blue-eyed slaves and asked the bystanders, 'Who are they?' On being told that they were Angli, he pithily quipped: *Non angli sed angeli* (not Angli but angels). Because of the different beauty of these fair young men under southern skies, a 'dear chance' came for England on that day, says the poet. The encounter prompted Gregory to send the first Christian missionaries, led by St Augustine (later Archbishop of Canterbury), to the English.

Our human response to beauty, even in 'block or barren stone', is ultimately a form of worship, but Hopkins wishes to say more. What most clearly mirrors God's better beauty, he says, is the human self, flashing 'off frame and face'. This is the beauty we must love and cherish. When we are home in our own hearts, we are free to own it, free to bless it and free to leave it, which means free to give beauty 'back to God, beauty's self and beauty's giver', as he wrote in 'The Leaden Echo, The Golden Echo'.

To what serves Mortal Beauty?

To what serves mortal beauty | —dangerous; does set danc-
ing blood—the O-seal-that-so | feature, flung prouder form
Than Purcell tune lets tread to? | See: it does this: keeps warm
Men's wits to the things that are; | what good means—where a glance
Master more may than gaze, | gaze out of countenance.
Those lovely lads once, wet-fresh | windfalls of war's storm,
How then should Gregory, a father, | have gleanèd else from swarm-
ed Rome? But God to a nation | dealt that day's dear chance.
To man, that needs would worship | block or barren stone,
Our law says: Love what are | love's worthiest, were all known;
World's loveliest—men's selves. Self | flashes off frame and face.
What do then? how meet beauty? | Merely meet it; own,
Home at heart, heaven's sweet gift; | then leave, let that alone.
Yea, wish that though, wish all, | God's better beauty, grace.

That Nature is a Heraclitean Fire and of the Comfort of Resurrection

WHAT HAS always attracted me to Hopkins is his realism, his respect for what *is*. He was a classical scholar, and in his poetry we get a distillation of the thought of the pre-Socratic philosopher of being, Parmenides. He writes: 'I have often felt … [about] the depths of the instress or how fast the inscape holds a thing that nothing is so pregnant and straightforward to the truth as simple *yes* and *is*.'[43] The *isness* of nature, of persons and of his own self, particularly in the Dark Sonnets, is passionately observed, seen, tasted, touched and deeply experienced. Such realism moves his poetry beyond vagueness, gives it an edge and an undying freshness and vigour.

We know that there is always a 'more' infusing Hopkins's apprehension of things, because he is a poet of the Incarnation. For him to truly attend to things and persons in their going as selves is also to inscape Christ who plays in all things. To return to the classical foundation of his aesthetics, however, I also learned that the *isness* that enthuses him is no flat monochrome *isness*. It is shaped by the antithesis of becoming, destruction, creativity and endless change. Thus, we also find included in this poem a distillation of another Greek thinker, Heraclitus, the sixth/fifth-century BC philosopher known as the 'philosopher of becoming'. For Heraclitus, the foundation of things is fire (meaning hot air); it is flux and the destruction of what is. Out of this destruction comes endless change and creativity.

Opinions have been put forward as to why Hopkins makes this surprising leap, and an obvious one is the influence of Darwinian evolution, where destruction and emergence are governing principles of the universe. I believe that the poet's experience of chaos and breakdown in his own life had also a part to play. It led him to see that this is how being (or creation) works in the Creator's hands, a view he embraced with courage and hope, as expressed in the Dark Sonnets. What he has lived through now becomes the base for a larger myth, an imaginative construct of how God deals with his creation as a whole. This rollicking poem is surprisingly celebratory, for another order is being created in which, paradoxically, *is* and *is not* are held together. This order, this 'new creation' (as St Paul designates it), is the order of Resurrection and it is God's action alone.

A first-time reader can get bogged down with the language in this poem. Though Hopkins knew that his poems needed explanation at times, he also believed that they should primarily be read or heard for the sound, rhythm and energy of the words. With such a trust we open ourselves to the special feat of imagination that meets us here. 'That Nature is a Heraclitean Fire and the Comfort of Resurrection' was composed in Dublin on 26 July 1888, a 'windy bright day'. It was also an extremely hot day, preceded and followed by floods or rain, 'a preposterous summer', as he wrote in correspondence at that time.[44] We are glad for the poet, for he seems to be on his way to a personal recovery. Looking to the sky above he writes of the clouds with energy and pleasure, how they flaunt each other, chase each other in the air like gangs of schoolboys out for the day. He is entranced by the effects of light on roughcast or dazzling whitewash, splintering behind elm arches ('Shivelights') and dancing with the shadows. The shadows lead his eyes downwards to earth, where he scans the parching effects of the hot air. Here he begins to be concerned about the human being. On this parched earth where will be the 'manmarks' of the ones who toiled on it? How can there be footprints when all moisture and wetness have stanched them away, and when all effects are mercilessly erased as 'nature's bonfire burns on'?

In the first turn of the sonnet he continues to describe the fate of the human being in this cosmic view. The poet's mood now is one of resistance, 'indignation' and lament, especially for the human in creation. He laments that this 'clearest-selved spark' of creation, the one with consciousness, 'disseveral, a star', distinct in his or her own uniqueness, whose 'firedint' leaves its mark on the universe at so many cultural levels, is just destined to be 'drowned' in an 'enormous dark'? The leveller, indeed the rogue, he says, in Heraclitus' universe, is death, blacker than black. Death beats all to its own level. Hopkins, frail in health at this time, both psychologically and physically, must have thought about his own death.

Then, in the sonnet's second turn, he makes another leap and suddenly proclaims:

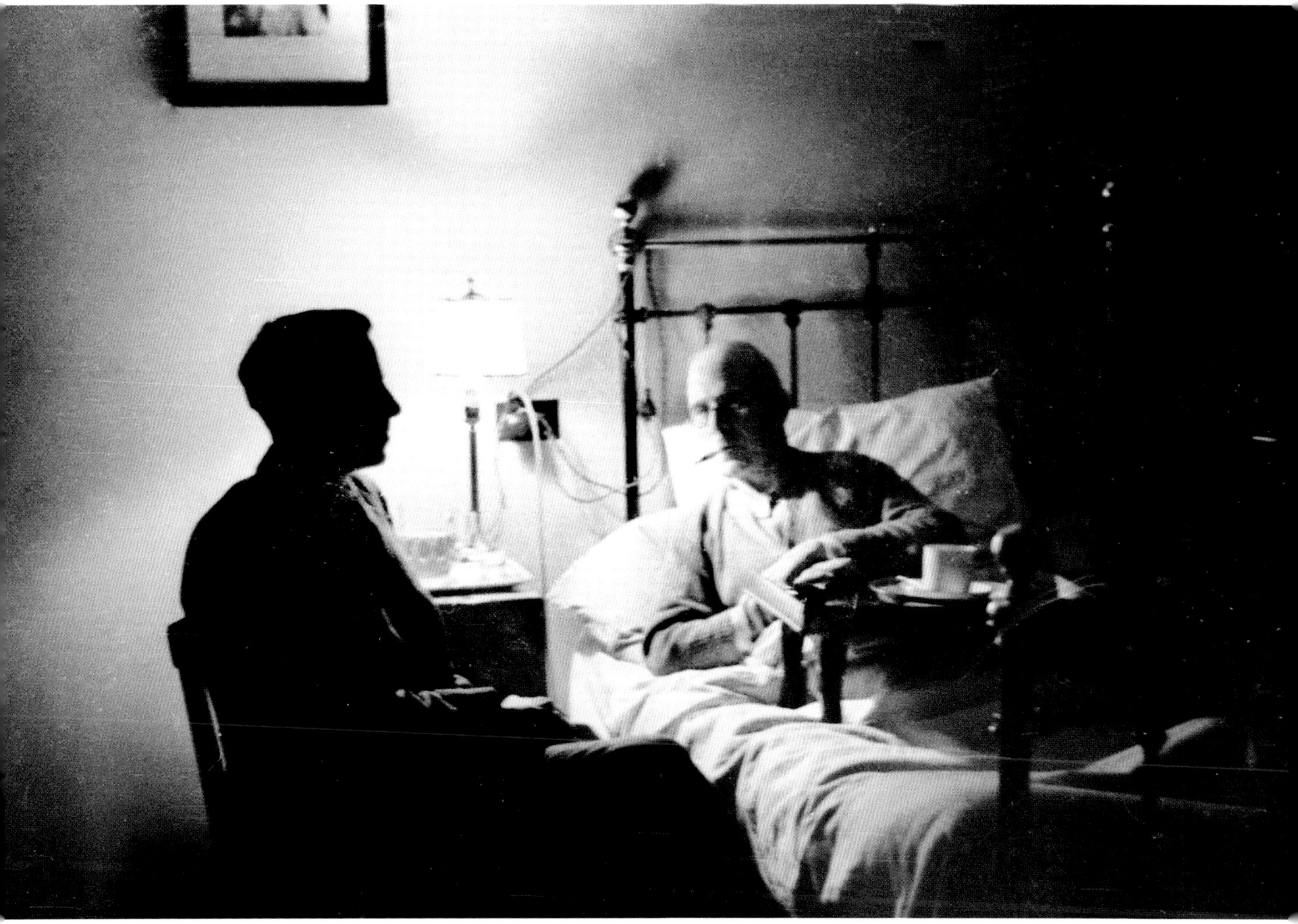

Fr Browne's brother, William, in St Vincent's Hospital, St Stephen's Green, Dublin (1938).

'Enough! the Resurrection'. He knows that creation and the human in no way in themselves can anticipate this new *more* of Resurrection. It is a pure gift of God. Echoing St Paul (1 Cor 15:51–52), the Resurrection truth rings like a clarion in his heart. To him, as to a joyless traveller foundering on the deck of a sinking ship, it is like a beacon of light from an 'eternal' or other order. (He may have the high moment of rescue in 'The Wreck of the Deutschland' in mind here). Having received this assurance, he now flaunts the accidental, shaming effects of death – the fading of flesh, the humiliation of being reduced to being food for worms. They no longer matter. Neither does it matter, he exclaims, that in life in his present body, (his 'bone-house, mean house' as he names it elsewhere), that he is a 'Jack' (a common fellow), a 'joke' (a laughing stock), 'poor potsherd' (like the shard with which Job scraped his sores), a 'patch' (a dolt), 'matchwood' (one who burns up immediately like insubstantial woodshavings)! It does not matter because now he has come to know that nothing of him will be wasted since he is also 'all at once what Christ is', Christ who was of the same flesh as him, and in whom his own unique self will live on in its transformed 'I am' beyond death. In Christ, he will be 'immortal diamond'.

Hopkins had just over ten months to live when he wrote this optimistic hymn to the permanence of the human self in the Resurrection. 'Immortal Diamond' was engraved on the memorial stone to Hopkins, which was unveiled on 8 December 1975 in the Poets' Corner of Westminster Abbey.

That Nature is a Heraclitean Fire and of the comfort of the Resurrection

Cloud-puffball, torn tufts, tossed pillows | flaunt forth, then chevy on an air–
built thoroughfare: heaven-roysterers, in gay-gangs | they throng; they glitter in marches.
Down roughcast, down dazzling whitewash, | wherever an elm arches,
Shivelights and shadowtackle in long | lashes lace, lance, and pair.
Delightfully the bright wind boisterous | ropes, wrestles, beats earth bare
Of yestertempest's creases; in pool and rut peel parches
Squandering ooze to squeezed | dough, crust, dust; stanches, starches
Squadroned masks and manmarks | treadmire toil there
Footfretted in it. Million-fuelèd, | nature's bonfire burns on.
But quench her bonniest, dearest | to her, her clearest-selvèd spark
Man, how fast his firedint, | his mark on mind, is gone!
Both are in an unfathomable, all is in an enormous dark
Drowned. O pity and indig | nation! Manshape, that shone
Sheer off, disseveral, a star, | death blots black out; nor mark
Is any of him at all so stark
But vastness blurs and time | beats level. Enough! the Resurrection,
A heart's-clarion! Away grief's gasping, | joyless days, dejection.
Across my foundering deck shone
A beacon, an eternal beam. | Flesh fade, and mortal trash
Fall to the residuary worm; | world's wildfire, leave but ash:
In a flash, at a trumpet crash,
I am all at once what Christ is, | since he was what I am, and
This Jack, joke, poor potsherd, | patch, matchwood, immortal diamond,
Is immortal diamond.

In Honour of St Alphonsus Rodriguez

THIS SONNET was ritten in October 1888. The first verse came to Hopkins while he was strolling through the Phoenix Park. He had been asked to compose a poem for 30 October, the feast day of the newly canonised Alphonsus Rodriguez, a Jesuit lay brother who served as a porter for forty years at the Jesuit house in Palma, Majorca. Sending it to Robert Bridges , he wrote: '"snorting", the sonnet "aims at being intelligible", so do not put it aside "for further neglect" but answer smart'.[45] It is a simpler sonnet than the previous one, but, like all the Dublin poems, it is a prayer from the lower register of his soul where he looks at himself standing before God. On that score, he surmises that Alphonsus has much to teach him.

During the Golden Age of Spain, honour was earned by men through bravery and gallantry in battle. They forged their glory not only by action but by retaining signs of gashed flesh and galled shield as mementos. Hopkins demurs in the first line with 'so we say', implying there is more to be said. In the turn, line 5, he agrees that we do find signs of battle on special people, for example on Christ's body and on the bodies of some of his martyrs, but with the word 'be' (line 6) he reminds us of 'the war within, the brand we wield / Unseen'. From this there is no 'hurtle' (noise), and of this the world is unaware. Yet God is always there and aware, says the poet, hewing (the old-English equivalent of the Hebrew *bara*, to create) 'mountain and continent', enabling the growth of living things, and especially of the human being, whose growth is gradual and from within – with 'trickling increment'. Then there is the surprise of the word 'crowd' in the next line, where we might expect the word 'crown'. Returning to Alphonsus, he tells us that the saint's life also was indeed crowded with a special kind of conquest. Although his life within the placid walls of a college on a beautiful and temperate island was outwardly uneventful, his spiritual life, as his extensive writings tell us, was quite intense, fraught with struggle and temptation, while, in strict obedience to his calling as porter, he simply 'watched the door'.

In the previous sonnet on Resurrection, Hopkins had stressed the final utter God-given transformation coming at the end; here he stresses the 'trickling increment',

Birds, Irish Sea, May 1941

day by day, of the experience itself. In his own life the poet believed that this included the main work assigned to him, which bothered him so, and the uneventful and grinding work of 'examining a nation.' It is possibly because of this work, undertaken in obedience, that he has empathy with this simple lay brother. In this fragile time he is still searching for answers, indeed for a way of managing his life, as he admits to Robert Bridges.[46] Does the simplicity of Alphonsus's way model for him how he might bring his own natural wilfulness into total dependence on God?

In Honour of St Alphonsus Rodriguez

Laybrother of the Society of Jesus upon the
first falling of his feast after his canonisation
For the College of Palma in the Island
Of Majorca, where the saint lived for
40 years as Hall porter

Honour is flashed off exploit, so we say;
And those strokes once that gashed flesh or galled shield
Should tongue that time now, trumpet now that field,
And, on the fighter, forge his glorious day.
On Christ they do and on the martyr may;
But be the war within, the brand we wield
Unseen, the heroic breast not outward-steeled,
Earth hears no hurtle then from fiercest fray.

Yet God (that hews mountain and continent,
Earth, all, out; who, with trickling increment,
Veins violets and tall trees makes more and more)
Could crowd career with conquest while there went
Those years and years by of world without event
That in Majorca Alfonso watched the door.

'Thou art indeed just, Lord'

THIS POWERFUL and plaintive poem is considered by some to be one of the Dark Sonnets, possibly because it shows Hopkins in questioning mode, although it is also haunted by a strange fitness for the end. It dates from 17 March 1889, and may have been written at Miss Cassidy's home in Monasterevin, by the 'burling Barrow brown', where he had come for a rest. He identifies with the prophet Jeremiah's complaint to God, as we note from the Latin epigraph to the poem, citing Jeremiah 12:1:

> You will be in the right [just], O Lord,
> when I lay charges against you;
> but let me put my case to you.
> Why does the way of the guilty prosper?

Some find in this poem a collapse, a giving in to despair. MacKenzie would have titled it 'Bitterness in Spring,' saying it is ironic that one of his most enduring poems should be based on the conviction that no work of his would ever endure.[47] I would not go so far. I think that Hopkins, by temperament, is given to either enthusiasm or pathos. And with his poor state of health in the year in which he died, these polarities are experienced more deeply.

In reading the Resurrection poem, we saw him in an exalted mood and setting foot on firm ground, knowing that as 'immortal diamond' nothing of him would by lost. In the light of the more contemplative spirituality of the newly canonised Alphonsus, we saw him responding to a method of managing his life with more equilibrium and peace. In Ignatian terms we may say that the experiences behind these two poems were times of consolation, and were important for his sense of self, in that they stimulated him to write. But experiences like these don't last, and in the current poem, the 'motionable', questioning mind of the poet again takes over. On the one hand we are led into the poem with the presiding text of Jeremiah, which accepts that a just God is in charge and then, on the other, we are faced with an argumentative poet who feels defeated, as he experiences the burgeoning life of spring all round him in Monasterevin. Just to live is a strain, since he, dried up, can no longer 'breed one work that wakes'. Natural creation, whether lusty or not, appears to thrive before the Creator, and he too, why is he not thriving? Even the common cow parsley – 'fretty chervil' – lacing the banks is shaken by the wind, but nothing shakes him. Everywhere is growth. 'Birds build – but not I build.' Thus, in his very essence/inscape – the source of his *poesis* or making of poems – he is being thwarted.

He brings the plea to God because he knows God is just. Like an advocate he first distances God with 'thou' and 'sir' in order to have the freedom to declare his rights. Even if you were my enemy, he says, you couldn't have done worse, but I know you are not, and then he changes to the tender word 'friend'. God as *just* and God as *friend*! His holding of these together is, I think, his response to the plea in the poem.

Some private notes made during his last retreat on New Year's Day 1889 are helpful here. He records how he entered into a course of loathing and hopelessness that he had felt before, and which had made him fear madness, and during that time he had given up meditation. On returning to meditation during this retreat, the self-loathing occurred again. All he could do was say to the Lord, 'Thou art indeed just', and be in the Lord's presence in his tiredness and inadequacy.[48] As the retreat notes make clear, he is letting go, indeed is forced to let go of the more linear discursive meditation he was trained in, for a simpler resting in God with one thought/phrase in a prayer of abiding or contemplation. (Regarding his spiritual life there are critics who say that the applied meditation of the earlier stages of the Spiritual Exercises exacerbated his scrupulous and perfectionistic temperament, who was always asking do I love God enough?).

However, I think the contemplative quality has always been there in Hopkins's poetry. In the exultant Welsh days all things in their inscapes spoke to him unambiguously of God as given in them, and so God is gloriously praised. In the Dublin sonnets, something new happens. He is still receiving, but now from a more ambiguous, even dark God. It seems that what draws this present poem together is the self-emptying acceptance of the Creator as both a just and loving friend. A simple

View of River Barrow (where Count John McCormack sang 'Song of my Heart'), Monasterevin, Kildare, New Year's Day, 1942

abiding in this truth is sufficient for him. Yet, finally, returning to the spring landscape again, we are back to the irrepressible poet who changes tactics and now addresses God as 'lord of life'. He prays 'send my roots rain', the force of the possessive 'mine' at the beginning extending to *my* 'lord', my 'life', *my* 'roots'. Ultimately, he knows that in the hands of the 'lord of Life', his life and his roots are safeguarded. He will never be obliterated. Never giving up on himself or on his special gift, he does not believe that God will do so either.

In conclusion to this selection, I cannot resist including a comment Hopkins once made to Robert Bridges. Writing of one of his compositions, he said: 'If the whole world agreed to see nothing in it I should only tell them to take a generation and come to me again'.[49] Indeed, he was prescient about how his poetry would be received, and we now know how right he was.

'Thou art indeed just, Lord'

Thou art indeed just, Lord, if I contend
With thee; but, sir, so what I plead is just.
Why do sinners' ways prosper? and why must
Disappointment all I endeavour end?

Wert thou my enemy, O thou my friend,
How wouldst thou worse, I wonder, than thou dost
Defeat, thwart me? Oh, the sots and thralls of lust
Do in spare hours more thrive than I that spend,

Sir, life upon thy cause. See, banks and brakes
Now leavèd how thick! lacèd they are again
With fretty chervil, look, and fresh wind shakes

Them; birds build—but not I build; no, but strain,
Time's eunuch, and not breed one work that wakes.
Mine, O thou lord of life, send my roots rain.

'Manhill' from the bows. Cobh, County Cork, 1930

Part Four

THE WRECK OF THE DEUTSCHLAND

The Wreck of the Deutschland

'THE WRECK of the Deutschland' is Hopkins's greatest poem and a substantial proof that he was a poet of genius. After a poetic silence of seven years, the poem came almost as a release. It was the first poem written at St Beuno's between late December 1875 and the following April. I place it at the end of the selection because it is the longest and most demanding of his works. It was not accepted for publication during his lifetime. Robert Bridges found the language impossibly contorted in light of the poetic style of the time. In 1918, twenty-nine years after his friend's death, Bridges edited the first complete publication of Hopkins's poems with the disclaimer on 'The Wreck of the Deutschland': 'the dragon at the gate that bars all entrance to later poems'. However, we know that dragons guard treasures, and when we stay with this great poem, we will find not only that it stands alone in its completeness, but, like a womb, seems to contain all Hopkins's later poems.

Many things combined to bring Hopkins to the point of breaking his poetic fast. There was the event of the sinking of a German passenger and cargo ship, *The Deutschland,* with the loss of sixty of the one hundred people on board, among them five Franciscan nuns who had been expelled from Germany because of the anti-clerical laws there. The ship was headed for the United States but came aground on hidden sandbanks at Kentish Knock at the entrance to the Thames estuary. The disaster occurred between midnight and morning of 7 December 1875.

Hopkins had obviously read the various accounts of the shipwreck in the newspapers and he was particularly affected by the death of the nuns. On noticing this the kindly rector, Fr James Jones, suggested that he write a poem about it. Wrecks were quite common then and the poet would have heard them spoken about around the family table as his father was a marine insurance adjuster. Yet, for Hopkins, this was more than just another wreck. The report that one of the five drowned Franciscan sisters had called out in the storm, 'Christ, come quickly', confirmed for him that there is an answer – a divine one – to all the travails of life, both large and personal. With an inner and outer movement, the factual narrative of events evokes the majestic and merciful presence of God.

Hopkins, a classical scholar, is considered to have modelled the style on one of the early Greek poets, Pindar, who celebrated the victories of the Greek athletes with poems of praise to the gods. Like Pindar, Hopkins treats his readers here to an ode, a liturgical poem that is ultimately a prayer of praise. He would have been aware of the two strains of thought that run together in a Greek ode – *the overthought*, which is factual and descriptive and which everybody can see and hear, and the *underthought*, which is conveyed chiefly by metaphor and is often only half realised by the poet himself. As we shall see, the metaphor for the underthought here is water. Water is everywhere, evoking the divine presence, 'winter and warm', at once majestic, destructive and purifying, yet also bathing with gentleness. Hopkins has attempted a lot in this poem; like Milton, he seeks to justify the ways of God to men.

The ode is in two parts: Part the First – Stanzas 1–10, and Part the Second, Stanzas 11–35. He first wrote the narrative part, beginning with the twelfth stanza. But he has insisted that the principal thrust of the poem is lyrical, since it is an ode rather than pure narrative, and also that it is autobiographical, especially in Part the First. At a time in his spiritual life he too felt 'wrecked' by what God was asking him, and throughout the poem he seeks an answer not only for the passengers of the doomed ship, but for his own self. Because the poet himself is so present in 'The Wreck of the Deutschland', the poem invites us to do more than read it; we have to live it.

Part the First

Stanzas 1–10

Stanza 1 The dramatic first lines assault us: 'Thou mastering me / God'. God is a nurturing 'breath and bread'. Aquatic and naval imagery abound and as ruler God is 'sway of the sea', the cross wind and the 'world's strand'. The dead as well as the living are under God's rule Like Job (in Job 1:21), the poet challenges the One who 'bound bones and veins' in him and 'fastened me flesh' (there are also hints of Psalm 139:13 here). Then he asks: is such dread action necessary that he might be remade again by the finger of God?

Stanza 2 In a letter written in August 1877 Hopkins told Bridges that the experience of being *unmade* is autobiographical, in the hope that his friend might give the poem a little more credence.[50] But whether the divine is 'lightning' or 'lashed rod', the poet knows his identity is never wiped out. Stanza 2 begins with the heartening first line: 'I did say yes', and goes on to recall a memory of a long retreat he made while in Roehampton and before leaving for St Beuno's to study for the priesthood. It was a particularly intense time before another milestone in his life. The record of it in a private journal entry of September 1873 speaks of a sense of falling: 'the body no longer swayed as a piece by the nervous and muscular instress seems to fall in and hang like a dead weight on the chest.'[51] He recalls it as a time of 'wrecking', and we notice how the language of the ship's wrecking is drawn upon to express it.

Stanza 3 In entanglements with the divine presence and in his suffering, he does not flee directly to the stern, frowning face of the Creator, but to where his heart, 'mother of being in me, heart' (Stanza 18), takes him. And it takes him 'with a fling of the heart to the heart of the Host'. He congratulates his heart, which, like a carrier-pigeon, knows how to go home, home to where divine mercy receives him. There is no desolation here, as in Stanzas 1–2. There is release. The poet's spirit towers like the nun when she calls to Christ as she perishes in the shipwreck.

The Wreck of the Deutschland

1

Thou mastering me
God! giver of breath and bread;
World's strand, sway of the sea;
Lord of living and dead;
Thou hast bound bones and veins in me, fastened me flesh,
And after it almost unmade, what with dread,
Thy doing: and dost thou touch me afresh?
Over again I feel thy finger and find thee.

2

I did say yes
O at lightning and lashed rod;
Thou heardst me truer than tongue confess
Thy terror, O Christ, O God;
Thou knowest the walls, altar and hour and night:
The swoon of a heart that the sweep and the hurl of thee trod
Hard down with a horror of height:
And the midriff astrain with leaning of, laced with fire of stress.

Stanza 4 We get a sense of the storm subsiding and a relative feeling of calm. Some time to think, maybe, and to ask 'who am I and where am I now?' Again, naval imagery abounds. Am I soft sand sifting in an hour-glass bound, fastened at a wall? Am I cut off, adrift, like the rudderless ship? I am all these, he says, but there is also in my motionable mind a steadiness and poise because of Christ's gift. Just as the Maenefa Hillock ('voel') and its rivulets shelter St Beuno's from the back, the poet also feels sheltered and supported ('roped') by a spring coming down from above. It is Christ's gift, the promise of the Gospel, which of its very nature is also a 'principle', bidding him as a disciple of Christ to rise up from dejection and to praise.

Stanza 5 Praise is what the poet does here. In this oft-cited, musical and softly lyrical piece, he is no longer in self-questioning mode. He simply experiences the consolation, which, as a disciple of St Ignatius, he knows God sometimes gives as encouragement. Like a lover he kisses his hand to the divine presence in the stars, not forgetting the times also when he must bless to understand. In 'The Wreck of the Deutschland' we are introduced to one of his newly coined words – 'instress', the correlative of 'inscape'. The sense in Stanza 5 is that when the inscape of divine beauty graciously opens itself to us, we must 'instress' it. We must savour it in our experience, and by word or action *stress* it in our lives.

Stanzas 6–8 Here there is a change of tone that presents us with a complex synthesis of Christian truths. As Aidan Nicholls says, Hopkins is the theologian's poet. One of his gifts is to open up for all peoples of faith new ways of seeing and wording the Christian mystery. In these stanzas we are invited to see how the 'selving' of God works itself out in the universe and in our lives.

Stanza 6 says the selving of God instresses us in many ways. Do not limit it by seeing it only as interventions from heaven to assuage human guilt with storms and earthquakes, or just the melting of our hearts as with the beauty of starlight (Stanza 5). Think of it rather as working itself out continuously in this world, where it 'rides time like riding a river'. For *the* divine stress in our world is the mystery of Incarnation in

3

The frown of his face
Before me, the hurtle of hell
Behind, where, where was a, where was a place?
I whirled out wings that spell
And fled with a fling of the heart to the heart of the Host.
My heart, but you were dovewinged, I can tell,
Carrier-witted, I am bold to boast,
To flash from the flame to the flame then, tower from the grace to the grace.

4

I am soft sift
In an hourglass—at the wall
Fast, but mined with a motion, a drift,
And it crowds and it combs to the fall;
I steady as a water in a well, to a poise, to a pane,
But roped with, always, all the way down from the tall
Fells or flanks of the voel, a vein

Of the gospel proffer, a pressure, a principle, Christ's gift.

5

I kiss my hand
To the stars, lovely-asunder
Starlight, wafting him out of it; and
Glow, glory in thunder;
Kiss my hand to the dappled-with-damson west:
Since, tho' he is under the world's splendour and wonder,
His mystery must be instressed, stressed;
For I greet him the days I meet him, and bless when I understand.

which God has chosen to be with us here, where we are – as creatures of earth. But, says the poet sadly, do we really accept Incarnation? Let us ask why not? Is it because it brings God in Christ too close?

Incarnation is a divine event in history, and in Stanzas 7 and 8, in story or ballad form, he outlines the main action of the most important truth the world has ever known. Indeed, Hopkins gives us a fresh way of understanding it. As we know, for him the self is always *act*: the 'self goes itself', he says in 'As Kingfishers Catch Fire'. The self of God *goes* in Jesus of Nazareth in Galilee. The grey womb of the maiden already presages the *going* of the dense and driven passion, the death and the grave, though the grave which is *warm* is not lifeless, and if we so desire our minds can run ahead to the Resurrection.

The images of flushing, melting, discharging swelling, flooding all refer to the peaking of energy released by Christ in the world. The river of this energy is ever in flood; was even anticipated in the Old Testament, is in flood at this moment, but it is up to us to *instress* it in our times.

There is no simple answer here as to how we appropriate this truth, but the poet, from his own experience, knows that 'only the heart, being hard at bay, / Is out with it'. We note the tension and energy here in the way the language is so structured that the reader must spring ahead from the last line of Stanza 7 to its outride in Stanza 8 to complete the sentence.

Stanza 8 pursues the theme that only a conflicted heart can truly give voice to God's Christ-presence in our world. As a poet, Hopkins goes on to give us an experience of the sheer shock of this knowing. He turns to nature for a parallel and we see how he juggles sharp consonants and single vowel sounds to describe the bitter taste of a sloe! We may not like the taste at first but it does flush us out! And because of the flush, we are fascinated and we try it again and again. It is the same, says Hopkins, in our relation to what the hero of Calvary has done for us. We don't like it at first; we think we don't need it and we resist. Then, over time, we cease to ask what it means and trusting our desire we go to Christ's feet.

6

Not out of his bliss
Springs the stress felt
Nor first from heaven (and few know this)
Swings the stroke dealt—
Stroke and a stress that stars and storms deliver,
That guilt is hushed by, hearts are flushed by and melt—
But it rides time like riding a river
(And here the faithful waver, the faithless fable and miss).

7

It dates from day
Of his going in Galilee;
Warm-laid grave of a womb-life grey;
Manger, maiden's knee;
The dense and the driven Passion, and frightful sweat;
Thence the discharge of it, there its swelling to be,
Though felt before, though in high flood yet—
What none would have known of it, only the heart, being hard at bay,

8

Is out with it! Oh,
We lash with the best or worst
Word last! How a lush-kept plush-capped sloe
Will, mouthed to flesh-burst,
Gush!—flush the man, the being with it, sour or sweet,
Brim, in a flash, full!—Hither then, last or first,
To hero of Calvary, Christ, 's feet—
Never ask if meaning it, wanting it, warned of it—men go.

Stanzas 9 and 10 are in keeping with the exalted nature of the ode form. Part the First ends with a lyrical prayer. It is a hymn in praise of the Trinity and the mastery and mercy of God. Like Donne, in 'Batter my heart, Three-personed God, for Thee', the poet begs God to flush us out of hiding and to wring from us our evil tendencies. Addressing the One who is beyond the sweet saying of our words, he says, You will do it in your way, because often it is in your darkness that you are most merciful. In Stanza 10 the prayer rises again on behalf of our 'dogged in den' selves. The poet expresses confidence that God will deal with us according to our needs and abilities – either suddenly, bringing about a change of will, as in St Paul on the way to Damascus, or, more gently, stealing through us like spring, as with St Augustine. The questioning and resistance of the dramatic opening line of *The Wreck* has subsided and the poet's final beautiful prayer of the last two lines is one of adoration.

Part the Second

Stanzas 11–19

Stanza 11 Leading into the narrative, Hopkins wakes us up to the omnipresence of Death. Capitalised and introduced abruptly, with the cacophonous sounds of banging drum and blaring bugle, the action of death is like a medieval dance. With many instruments, it can rip through protective barriers of 'flange' and 'rail'; can show its 'fang' like a wild animal. Like a scythe it can 'cringe' us, lop us off and plough ('share') through us in indiscriminate 'blear' fashion. And all the while 'we dream we are rooted in earth – Dust!' and 'Wave with the meadow' of the mass of humanity. The manner of death is uncertain, but the end – unmaking – is not. Thus the poet establishes a tone with which we can all empathise, for no one escapes death.

Stanza 12 reads like a sea shanty, and we get a sense that the majority of passengers on board were setting out in hope to start a new life. The stanza mimics the speeding movement of the ship, and it is possible that the poet, on reading *The Times* on

9

Be adored among men,
God, three-numberèd form;
Wring thy rebel, dogged in den,
Man's malice, with wrecking and storm.
Beyond saying sweet, past telling of tongue,
Thou art lightning and love, I found it, a winter and warm;
Father and fondler of heart thou hast wrung:
Hast thy dark descending and most art merciful then.

10

With an anvil-ding
And with fire in him forge thy will
Or rather, rather then, stealing as Spring
Through him, melt him but master him still:
Whether at once, as once at a crash Paul,
Or as Austin, a lingering-out sweet skill,
Make mercy in all of us, out of us all
Mastery, but be adored, but be adored King.

Part the Second

11

'Some find me a sword; some
The flange and the rail; flame,
Fang, or flood' goes Death on drum,
And storms bugle his fame.
But we dream we are rooted in earth—Dust!
Flesh falls within sight of us, we, though our flower the same,
Wave with the meadow, forget that there must
The sour scythe cringe, and the blear share come.

Saturday, 11 December 1875, had in mind the criticisms around the disaster and the rapidity with which the captain forged ahead despite the storm and poor visibility, which led to the ship's foundering on the dangerous sandbanks. Sixty people died, their 'goal' now a 'shoal' or sandbank. A trite internal rhyme of words, perhaps, or, as Aidan Nicholls points out, does it accentuate the macabre disparity between expectations and what transpired?[52] Writing in pre-ecumenical times the poet is aware that there are many on the ship who are not under the wings ('feathers') of the Father (see Matthew 23:37). Nevertheless, drawing on an architectural image, he entrusts them to the not fully known dark depths of the bay of divine blessing, and conveys the hope that God in his mercy, who draws millions to himself, will in a way known only to him draw them also.

Stanza 13 The rapidity of movement, the sound and alliteration of consonants in this fine stanza mimic the apocalyptic nature of the disaster. And Hopkins is human in his observations: there will be women left without husbands and children without fathers.

Stanza 14 describes the disaster at Kentish Knock, a ridged sandbank notoriously perilous to shipping, twenty miles east of Harwich. It tells of the ship resisting and then collapsing, because the compass is now useless to the crew. Nor are the canvas, 'the whorl' (propeller) or the ship's wheel of any help, for she cannot be 'wafted' (floated), nor can she be set going by the wind.

Stanza 15 The tone changes here as the people on board wait with foreboding. The rhythm and diction conspire to say their hope is running out. Hopkins imagines hope as an old woman whose face is trenched with tears and carved with care and is already wearing her mourning garments. The ship was stranded at about five o'clock on the morning of 6 December, and all day, until five in the evening when darkness set in, the passengers looked for some signs of rescue. But visibility was poor and no help was sent out in the dangerous storm; when it did come, many lives had already

12

On Saturday sailed from Bremen,
American-outward-bound,
Take settler and seamen, tell men with women,
Two hundred souls in the round—
O Father, not under thy feathers nor ever as guessing
The goal was a shoal, of a fourth the doom to be drowned;
Yet did the dark side of the bay of thy blessing
Not vault them, the million of rounds of thy mercy not reeve even them in?

13

Into the snows she sweeps,
Hurling the haven behind,
The Deutschland, on Sunday; and so the sky keeps,
For the infinite air is unkind,
And the sea flint-flake, black-backed in the regular blow,
Sitting Eastnortheast, in cursed quarter, the wind;
Wiry and white-fiery and whirlwind-swivellèd snow
Spins to the widow-making unchilding unfathering deeps.

14

She drove in the dark to leeward,
She struck—not a reef or a rock
But the combs of a smother of sand: night drew her
Dead to the Kentish Knock;
And she beat the bank down with her bows and the ride of her keel:
The breakers rolled on her beam with ruinous shock;
And canvas and compass, the whorl and the wheel
Idle for ever to waft her or wind her with, these she endured.

literally been washed overboard. Finally, at nightfall, the desperate climbed into the sails, and clung there in the freezing air, the sails fast becoming their shrouds.

Stanza 16 Hopkins loves heroes. He recalls a newspaper account of one such man, roped to the rigging above, and how he leaped down to save a woman below on deck. Pitched to his death, his body was left headless, swinging to and fro. Hopkins admired physical courage and shows of strength (cf. 'The Soldier' and 'Felix Randal'), but here, though discreet in description, he seems fascinated that this 'handy and brave' man with 'dreadnought breast and braids of thew', should be sported about like a plaything by the powers of nature.

Stanza 17 There is another hero, however – this time a heroine. The pace of the poem moves quickly as Hopkins continues to present the facts with compression, crushing words together as the deck crushes its victims. The remarkable power of this stanza lies in the implied personification of Night in line 5 with the implication that there was Someone listening to the 'heart-broke rabble' with a 'heart-break hearing'. Still reticent about naming the Someone, Hopkins leaves it to his heroine. He introduces her as a prophetess, seeing her like the prophets of Israel who were 'the watchtowers' of the people, who could always be trusted to speak with 'virginal' and unadulterated tongues because they spoke words only from God, and so words that could be trusted to bring meaning to any disaster.

Stanza 18 gives us a moment of respite. In this beautiful and lyrical stanza we have the privilege of listening to the private Hopkins conversing with himself. Amazed, even embarrassed by his tears, he reflects that in the deepest reaches of his being is the heart, the 'mother of being' in him. He is discovering almost with joy that the heart, even in its tears, knows. Still cautious, he raises a few objections. He recalls the reminder of the prophet Jeremiah that the heart can be deceitful (Jer 17:9); and then, those embarrassing tears – are they still a welling up in him of youthful feelings, and are they more appropriate to the writing of a sweet madrigal? He discounts

15

Hope had grown grey hairs,
Hope had mourning on,
Trenched with tears, carved with cares,
Hope was twelve hours gone;
And frightful a nightfall folded rueful a day
Nor rescue, only rocket and lightship, shone,
And lives at last were washing away:
To the shrouds they took,—they shook in the hurling and horrible airs.

16

One stirred from the rigging to save
The wild woman-kind below,
With a rope's end round the man, handy and brave—

He was pitched to his death at a blow,
For all his dreadnought breast and braids of thew:
They could tell him for hours, dandled the to and fro
Through the cobbled foam-fleece, what could he do

With the burl of the fountains of air, buck and the flood of the wave?

17

They fought with God's cold—
And they could not and fell to the deck
(Crushed them) or water (and drowned them) or rolled
With the sea-romp over the wreck.
Night roared, with the heart-break hearing a heart-broke rabble,
The woman's wailing, the crying of child without check—
Till a lioness arose breasting the babble,
A prophetess towered in the tumult, a virginal tongue told.

these objections because of the 'glee' he is feeling. Glee is an unusual word, and in Hopkins's use of it, it means joy. The prophetess has touched his heart here with more than a private answer for his searching self. She has raised a larger truth, a truth for the heart and for all human suffering. Surpassing the self's narrow needs this divine truth is a truth of grace, hence the note of freedom and joy in 'glee'. In the next stanzas Hopkins tells us who this prophetess is and the rest of the poem never loses sight of her nor of the word she proclaims.

Stanza 19 A core insight on the prophetess is given in this stanza which begins with the word 'Sister'. She is a nun, and so a sister, but *it* could also mean that the poet finds in her a spiritual sister, in the way she calls on her master and his. The storm still rages on. Blinded by the 'rash smart sloggering brine', she is still able to see one thing; she has one 'fetch' in her to hear the truth from 'divine / Ears' and call it out to the survivors 'over the storm's brawling'. 'Fetch' is a seafaring term, meaning strategy or plan for directing a boat.

Stanzas 20–29 In Stanzas 20–23, Hopkins continues to build up slowly to the sister who, in the midst of the tumult, 'has one fetch in her', and who 'rears herself to divine / Ears'. He reflects historically on her as one of five German nuns of a Franciscan congregation. Because he does so with an elaborate and ornamental symbolism that diverges from the overall thrust of the ode, these stanzas appear contrived and even unnecessary, according to some critics. Sometimes the poet is unable to rein in his enthusiasms. He obviously has a great love for St Francis of Assisi, and he cannot resist giving us a small poem on Francis within the larger poem. This inclusion tells us a little more about Hopkins' strong sacramental sensibility and the richness of the word hoard he draws upon.

Stanza 20 *Deutschland* is the name of the doomed ship and of the sisters' homeland. Written 1875, this poem predated the later hostility between England and Germany. As we have seen, Hopkins writes with a faith view as a newly minted Catholic but he is

18

Ah, touched in your bower of bone
Are you! turned for an exquisite smart,
Have you! make words break from me here all alone,
Do you!—mother of being in me, heart.
O unteachably after evil, but uttering truth,
Why, tears! is it? tears; such a melting, a madrigal start!
Never-eldering revel and river of youth,
What can it be, this glee? the good you have there of your own?

19

Sister, a sister calling
A master, her master and mine!—
And the inboard seas run swirling and hawling;

The rash smart sloggering brine
Blinds her; but she that weather sees one thing, one;
Has one fetch in her: she rears herself to divine
Ears, and the call of the tall nun
To the men in the tops and the tackle rode over the storm's brawling.

20

She was first of a five and came
Of a coifèd sisterhood.
(O Deutschland, double a desperate name!
O world wide of its good!
But Gertrude, lily, and Luther, are two of a town,
Christ's lily and beast of the waste wood:
From life's dawn it is drawn down,
Abel is Cain's brother and breasts they have sucked the same.)

also limited by the pre-ecumenical mentality of his time. *Deutschland* was a *desperate* name, not only of the doomed ship, but also of Germany, the country in which, in the sixteenth century, the Reformation, that divided Christendom, originated. He then muses on the fact that a small German town, Eisleben, could give birth to two such contrasting persons: the fifteenth-century saint and mystic, St Gertrude the Great, 'Christ's lily', and the friar turned reformer, Martin Luther, the 'beast of the waste wood'. Hopkins would not have been aware of the theological depth of Luther's teaching which is more appreciated today across the Christian churches, but he would have been influenced by descriptions, extant in his time, of the friar and biblical scholar, who was coarse and offensive in language, especially with those with whom he did not agree. The poet continues to muse that such contrasts have been there from the beginning of time, as with Cain and Abel, both nurtured at the same breast, yet Cain became the murderer of his blameless shepherd brother.

Stanza 21 By a perverted irony, under Bismarck's regime the Catholic sisters were 'loathed' for their service to the German people and sent into exile. The Rhine and the Thames and the storm contributed to their deaths. However, these factors are but the hunting dogs of the constellation Orion the Hunter, symbol of Christ-Orion, the hunter of souls and hearts. He, the 'martyr-master', weighing their worth, chose them and took them from the sanctuary of their convent chapel for a wider public testing and witness. Christ-Orion looked down on them and in his regard, the 'Storm-flakes were scroll-leaved flowers … ', signs of 'sweet heaven' awaiting them.

Stanza 22 finds special significance in the fact that there were *five* sisters, for it is a sacred number which, from medieval times, in the cinquefoil windows of churches, drew the mind to Christ's sacrifice on the cross. And so it is a 'cipher' of the 'sake' or essence of Christ. ('Sake' is a Hopkins-coined word that conveys what is distinctive about a person.) And what is distinctive about Christ is the 'mark' of the five wounds, a mark made humanly and physically on his body, and speaking of 'Sacrifice [d]'. Even from the beginning the five sisters were 'his own bespoken', his chosen ones,

21

Loathed for a love men knew in them,
Banned by the land of their birth,

Rhine refused them. Thames would ruin them;
Surf, snow, river and earth
Gnashed: but thou art above, thou Orion of light;
Thy unchancelling poising palms were weighing the worth,
Thou martyr-master: in thy sight
Storm flakes were scroll-leaved flowers, lily showers—sweet heaven was astrew in them.

22

Five! the finding and sake
And cipher of suffering Christ.
Mark, the mark is of man's make
And the word of it Sacrificed.
But he scores it in scarlet himself on his own bespoken,
Before-time-taken, dearest prizèd and priced—
Stigma, signal, cinquefoil token
For lettering of the lamb's fleece, ruddying of the rose-flake.

23

Joy fall to thee, father Francis,
Drawn to the Life that died;
With the gnarls of the nails in thee, niche of the lance, his
Lovescape crucified
And seal of his seraph-arrival! and these thy daughters
And five-livèd and leavèd favour and pride,
Are sisterly sealed in wild waters,
To bathe in his fall-gold mercies, to breathe in his all-fire glances.

destined by their deaths to manifest in their bodies the 'scarlet' of sacrifice, scarlet being the martyrs' colour. With the same intensity he reminds us that martyrdom for saints does not occur by accident, but originates with the Lamb, the 'martyr-master'. The scarlet wounds are his 'stigma', his 'cinquefoil token' (the five-leaved rose being the traditional symbol of martyrdom) – all signs of what brands his fleece as Redeemer.

Stanza 23 With some relief and with joy he now turns to St Francis, the most Christ-like saint in the story of the Church, the spiritual father of the exiled nuns, and a saint whose life has been always seen as clearly and simply presenting Christ to us. Hopkins pays homage to him; he says you too were 'drawn to the life that died', to Christ on the Cross. He recalls how Francis's calling was sealed in a vision of a flaming seraph on Mount Alverna, in which he received the stigmata, the brand of the five wounds which identified him closely to Christ as 'Lovescape crucified'. Now he sees the five sisters in the same light also. Instead of the flaming seraph, it is the 'wild waters' which 'sisterly' seals them as they die together as a five-leaved cinquefoil. The exaltation and beauty of the final two lines are in a language of sacramental mysticism in which the 'wild waters' become their seal, their re-lettering, as now belonging to the divine 'lovescape'.

Stanza 24 Hopkins again takes a break to converse with himself and we are away with him in his beloved Wales. Feeling guilty at the ease of his own life amid such loss of life in the Thames Estuary, his spirit lifts on reading a variety of accounts of one of the sisters, his heroine, the 'tall nun'. Reports have varied, but it seems that in one last effort she raised herself through a deck opening and was calling 'O Christ, Christ, come quickly'. There is no more she could have done, marvels the poet. She has called the cross and Christ to her; she 'christens her wildworst Best' for the suffering throng around her, for herself, and for us all. 'Best' is capitalised by the poet, who is overwhelmed.

24

Away in the loveable west,
On a pastoral forehead of Wales,
I was under a roof here, I was at rest,
And they the prey of the gales;
She to the black-about air, to the breaker, the thickly
Falling flakes, to the throng that catches and quails
Was calling 'O Christ, Christ, come quickly':
The cross to her she calls Christ to her, christens her wild-worst Best.

25

The majesty! what did she mean?
Breathe, arch and original Breath.
Is it love in her of the being as her lover had been?
Breathe, body of lovely Death.
They were else-minded then, altogether, the men
Woke thee with a we are perishing in the weather of Gennesareth.
Or is it that she cried for the crown then,
The keener to come at the comfort for feeling the combating keen?

26

For how to the heart's cheering
The down-dugged ground-hugged grey
Hovers off, the jay-blue heavens appearing
Of pied and peeled May!
Blue-beating and hoary-glow height; or night, still higher,
With belled fire and the moth-soft Milky Way,
What by your measure is the heaven of desire,
The treasure never eyesight got, nor was ever guessed what for the hearing?

Stanza 25 begins with an exclamation on the 'majesty' of her utterance, and he asks 'what did she mean?' The next three stanzas are variable reflections on what she might mean, each of which he discards until he comes to the meaning in Stanza 28, which is the climax of the poem. He calls for inspiration from the Holy Spirit, the 'arch and original Breath' who breathed over the chaos of creation; he calls on the Son of God in his 'body of lovely Death' to help him. Could her sheer love for Jesus, her Bridegroom, have led her to utter the redeeming words? Not enough, he says: see how the disciples woke him with a 'we are perishing' in the storm on the boat. Or was it that she desired the honour of martyrdom, feeling that even with her pain it might be her due?

Stanza 26 And did she desire heaven? he asks. Unexpectedly, with a compression of colour and sound he lets the elements of nature evoke for us heavenly moments of release that she must have felt in her life as we do sometimes. But the desire to be in a heaven like this was not what shaped her words, the poet says, and anyway St Paul reminds us that we do not really know what heaven is like: the 'treasure' which 'no eye has seen, no ear has heard, what no mind of man can visualise that God has prepared for those who love him'(1 Cor 2:9).

Stanza 27 The nun and her predicament somehow fade out of the scene. Here the poet is not speaking of the critical life-versus-death moment that was hers, but the slow ebbing away of life as we know it because of 'The jading and jar of the cart'. He seems to speak about himself here, of the 'sheer plod' that is his existence (cf. 'The Windhover'), and the 'sweating' self he must endure at times (cf. 'I Wake and Feel'*)*. In such a situation, with spiritual training, one might take the edge of the isolation by turning one's thoughts to the Passion of Christ. But even this was not what was happening for her. 'Other' is the word he offers as 'measure' of her mind.

Stanaz 28 The poet is overwhelmed. The broken, staccato utterances read as coming from somebody in a crowd struggling to get to the front for a good view. He begs

27

No, but it was not these.
The jading and jar of the cart,
Time's tasking, it is fathers that asking for ease
Of the sodden-with-its-sorrowing heart,
Not danger, electrical horror; then further it finds
The appealing of the Passion is tenderer in prayer apart:
Other, I gather, in measure her mind's
Burden, in wind's burly and beat of endragonèd seas.

28

But how shall I ... make me room there:
Reach me a ... Fancy, come faster—
Strike you the sight of it? look at it loom there,
Thing that she ... there then! the Master,
Ipse, the only one, Christ, King, Head:
He was to cure the extremity where he had cast her;
Do, deal, lord it with living and dead;
Let him ride, her pride, in his triumph, despatch and have
done with his doom there.

29

Ah! there was a heart right!
There was single eye!
Read the unshapeable shock night

And knew the who and the why;
Wording it how but by him that present and past,
Heaven and earth are word of, worded by?—
The Simon Peter of a soul! to the blast
Tarpeian-fast, but a blown beacon of light.

for help. 'Fancy, come faster', he says, and while some commentators decry 'fancy' as a weak word, yet in its neo-Platonist origins as used by Hopkins, it designates a spiritual faculty akin to imagination. What is it the nun saw, he asks; let me have the images, the wording for it? And the words he uses, such as 'Sight of it', 'loom there' and 'Thing', have the objectivity about them, as does the climactic Latin word '*Ipse*', which means 'He himself'. This objectivity has led to various interpretations of the stanza, including one which says that Christ must have actually appeared personally to the nun and that her privileged encounter was the reason for the poet's great interest in her.[53] I rather think that with the realism of words like 'Thing' and '*Ipse*', Hopkins has in mind the objectivity of pure faith which is not limited by human sensibilities as described in Stanzas 25–27, and even transcends the human terror of drowning and death. This is faith in the Old Testament sense of the Hebrew *aman*, which means strength, firmness and complete reliance on the dependability of God, for 'she rears herself to divine / Ears' (Stanza 19). It is also faith in the New Testament sense that the God who is incarnate in Christ is Master, King, Head and a presence in the very materiality of the world itself, whether in peace and calm or in shipwreck and ruin. Christ's very presence would cure the extremity in which he had cast her. Hopkins boldly prays – 'Get on with it, Lord', You who 'ride[s] time like riding a river' (Stanza 6), this is your moment of triumph, the triumph of your grace in this woman. And we hope her reading of the storm as encounter with you will mollify your judgment on the many doomed who do not have that hope.

Stanza 29 Hopkins continues to praise the nun with her 'heart right' and 'single eye' for uttering the word that gave shape to the disaster. For she knows who Christ is, and that he, the Divine Word, is the real meaning of all things. Hopkins is particularly partial to this Johannine understanding of Christ as Word, the Word who was with the Creator from the beginning of time giving shape to things, and he sees his own poetry as participating in the mission of the Word in the universe. Not only does the nun, his

Nuns behind their 'grille' at the Presentation Convent, Listowel, Kerry, 1944

heroine, also bring shape to the 'unshapeable' with her word, but she, like St Peter, is a rock-like soul, immovable and firm in her faith as the Tarpeian cliff (later called the Capitoline), which symbolises the Catholic Church. On her likes, as on Peter, our faith can depend.

Stanzas 30–35

Stanza 30 After the intensity of the previous stanza, this one opens in a mood of gentleness and playfulness. Inspired by the synchronicity of dates, the poet reflects on the fact that the ship was in the throes of wreckage on the eve of the Feast of the Immaculate Conception of Mary. Of the nun, he says she is the model for Christians, in that she renews Incarnation in time. She shadowed Mary in hearing the Word made flesh, keeping him with heart love and assent of faith ('brain') and then uttering him into the watery chaos.

Stanza 31 In pain and patience, she has reached her reward, but what of the many others, especially the 'unconfessed of them'? Hopkins's newly accepted Catholicism does not oblige him to take a restrictive view of salvation. Calling to mind the psalmist on how God rescues us and covers us with his pinions and shelters us under his wings (Ps 91:3f), and the words of Jesus in the face of rejection by Jerusalem, how he longed to gather her children as a hen gathers her chicks under her wing (Mt 23:37), he confidently asserts that in this case the nun has been the bell to ring out the breadth of God's providential care, and to '[S]tartle the poor sheep back!' Switching to another metaphor, he says that maybe the shipwreck was God's way of harvesting more grains for the eternal barn?

Stanza 32 This is the first of two solemn stanzas of praise which evoke once again the mastery and mercy of God as announced in Part One. Here we experience poetry as heightened speech, as the language of an ode should be. Water once again stands for the undertow of wreck, death and fear of death. But we need not fear. Hopkins's God, like Job's, is master, and sets bounds to the power of the waters (Job 26:10). We

30

Jesu, heart's light,
Jesu, maid's son,
What was the feast followed the night
Thou hadst glory of this nun?—
Feast of the one woman without stain.
For so conceivèd, so to conceive thee is done;
But here was heart-throe, birth of a brain,
Word, that heard and kept thee and uttered thee outright.

31

Well, she has thee for the pain, for the
Patience; but pity of the rest of them!
Heart, go and bleed at a bitterer vein for the
Comfortless unconfessed of them—
No not uncomforted: lovely-felicitous Providence
Finger of a tender of; O of a feathery delicacy, the breast of the
Maiden could obey so, be a bell to, ring of it, and
Startle the poor sheep back! is the shipwrack then a harvest, does
tempest carry the grain for thee?

32

I admire thee, master of the tides,
Of the Yore-flood, of the year's fall;
The recurb and the recovery of the gulf's sides,
The girth of it and the wharf of it and the wall;
Stanching, quenching ocean of a motionable mind;
Ground of being, and granite of it: past all
Grasp God, throned behind
Death with a sovereignty that heeds but hides, bodes but abides;

cannot but admire him. With nautical language, the poet shows how the same God who irrigated the earth with the great flood at the beginning of time sets limits to the power of water. In the last four lines the poet is more personal and speaks of his own need for divine help to ease the agitation of his 'motional mind' (Stanza 4). But he can find rest in the majesty of this 'past all / Grasp God' as the very foundation of his being. He is the sovereign presence beyond our greatest human fear – death. Hidden, yet totally aware of us, as sovereign master he commands, and patiently, because he is mercy, bides time for our response.

Stanza 33 is praise of the divine mercy. The focus of the poet is on Christ as mercy's manifestation, and the richness of the language mirrors the complex density of the mystery. With a mercy that 'outrides / The all of water', Christ, recalling the ark of 'the Yore-flood', has ridden time from the beginning and has been a refuge for all kinds of penitents. Not only does he embrace the 'listener', but also the 'lingerer' of weak faith. There is no end to which his mercy will not go 'in the storm of his strides'. It will go to the 'uttermost mark' (a nautical term meaning buoy or beacon) to reach the souls in purgatory or the many outside the Christian dispensation. The poet who is attracted to the imaginative concreteness of Catholic truth is touching here on a rather neglected doctrine that is professed in the Creed – 'He descended into Hell'. We do not hear of it much today, but it is the belief that Christ after his death descended into the underworld to take back Adam, the prophets and saints of Israel and the mediocre souls pent in prison. The liturgy for this remembrance is still prayed in some churches on Holy Saturday. In the final powerful lines Hopkins likens Christ to an Atlantean figure, somewhat like the Christ of 'Hurrahing in Harvest', who holds the world on his shoulders. As the compassion of the Father, Christ has only one 'fetch' (strategy) in him, to empty himself in love and to embrace humanness in all its dimensions. But Hopkins, the moralist, reminds us that we have a part to play in our salvation. There is an 'uttermost mark' beyond which even Christ cannot go because we set the limit with our final 'yes' or 'no'.

On the way to Doon church, Kerry, in the snow, 1945

Stanza 34 Having uttered prayers of praise to the majesty and mercy of God, the poet now entrusts the needs of his homeland to him in prayer of petition in the final stanzas. He praises the incarnate Word of 'the doubled-natured name' of God-man, the antithesis of 'the double and desperate name' of the *Deutschland.* He who was 'heaven flung', of God only, and who was 'heart-fleshed' in Mary as her 'Miracle-in-Mary-of-flame', he, the middle one of the Trinity: he begs him to come not in frightening judgment as on the last day, nor as darkly or hiddenly as at his birth (see Stanza 7), but to come 'Kind' as to his kin, and like a king to claim his kinsmen as his own. If we indulge Hopkins's tendency to give multiple meaning to words, 'Kind' may also mean a plea to Christ come gently and persuasively, without blame, like a summer shower bringing renewal to 'the shire', his country. It is possible here that 'shire' refers to the more inclusive Britain, for the poet was in Wales and identified with it when he wrote the ode.

Stanza 35 Hopkins addresses the nun directly as 'Dame', an honorific applied to noblewomen and often used of professed nuns in those days. His use of 'our' and 'us' hints at his awareness that British negligence had a part to play in her death, but he also implies the larger significance of the event for his country. When he prays, 'Remember us in the roads', he may simply have in mind the Jesuit mission, but it is also possible that he is drawing on the literal naval meaning of roads as a protected space where ships are safely at anchor. As a Jesuit, never ceasing to be on mission himself, he turns to the nun, now in her safe heavenly space, to exert her influence to restore Britain once again to the protection of her King, as Britain once knew him in pre-Reformation days. And then he prays the simply beautiful Easter Prayer – 'Let him easter in us'. Let Christ be a bright dawn that clears away our dimness, and just as the 'crimson-cresseted east' gave hope to the survivors on the ship when they saw the clouds being touched by the rising sun and lighting up the little crosses on beacons on the horizon, so let Christ once again give us hope and brighten Britain. The last two lines are a forceful recapitulation of the way in which the incarnate Word has been spoken of in the ode. The compression of titles of Christ, when read

33

With a mercy that outrides
The all of water, an ark
For the listener; for the lingerer with a love glides
Lower than death and the dark;
A vein for the visiting of the past-prayer, pent in prison,
The-last-breath penitent spirits—the uttermost mark
Our passion-plungèd giant risen,
The Christ of the Father compassionate, fetched in the storm of his strides.

34

Now burn, new born to the world,
Doubled-naturèd name,
The heaven-flung, heart-fleshed, maiden-furled
Miracle-in-Mary-of-flame,
Mid-numbered He in three of the thunder-throne!
Not a dooms-day dazzle in his coming nor dark as he came;
Kind, but royally reclaiming his own;
A released shower, let flash to the shire, not a lightning of fire hard-hurled.

35

Dame, at our door
Drowned, and among our shoals,
Remember us in the roads, the heaven-haven of the Reward:
Our King back, oh, upon English souls!
Let him easter in us, be a dayspring to the dimness of us, be a
crimson-cresseted east,
More brightening her, rare-dear Britain, as his reign rolls,
Pride, rose, prince, hero of us, high-priest,
Our hearts' charity's hearth's fire, our thoughts' chivalry's throng's Lord.

aloud, sound like the echo of a drum-roll and the surge of the ocean. He is our Pride, rose, prince, hero of us, high priest. He must become once again the fire of charity in British 'hearths' (homes) and hearts, the One to whom our noblest thoughts are addressed. The ode ends where it began, with God, but now with fuller joy and praise at having understood an event that had threatened to unmake him. The masterful and merciful God we meet in the opening of the poem is also the 'Lord', the incarnate One who rides with us through the disasters of time (Stanza 6).

Francis Browne SJ

Photographer

Francis Browne SJ

Photographer

Adapted from The Life and Lens of Father Browne *by E E O'Donnell SJ*

Francis Mary Hegarty Browne, the youngest of eight children, was born in the Sunday's Well, Cork in 1880. He came from a well-to-do family who lived in a substantial house on Buxton Hill. James Browne, Frank's father, was in the milling as well as the tanning business. Sadly, his mother died a few days after he was born, and his father in a swimming accident at Crosshaven in 1898. With both parents deceased, his uncle Robert, Bishop of Cloyne, took him under his wing, and was to become one of the most influential people in Frank Browne's life.

Frank Browne's secondary education took place at Belevdere College, a Jesuit school in Dublin, and at Castleknock College, and was completed with a Grand Tour of Europe in 1897. Equipped with a Kodak camera, he travelled with his brother William through France, Italy, Switzerland and Germany. These first photographs, taken on this trip at the age of seventeen, already show signs of the expertise that was to follow.

On his return from the Continent, on 7 September 1897, Frank Browne entered the Society of Jesus at its novitiate in Tullabeg, near Tullamore in County Offaly. On arrival, Frank had to surrender his camera as a 'superfluity'. For three years beginning in the autumn of 1899, 'Mister' Frank Browne was a student of the Royal University of Ireland at St Stephen's Green, Dublin. This was the University College founded by Cardinal Newman where Gerard Manley Hopkins SJ had been Professor of Greek until his death in 1889. Frank studied Greek there, as well as Latin and English. He had a classmate called James Joyce, who later in life featured him in his book *Finnegans Wake* as 'Mr Browne the Jesuit'. Upon graduation, Frank was sent to study philosophy for three years at Chieri in Northern Italy.

It was at this time that he began to study Italian painting seriously and he photographed many masterpieces on a systemic basis. While studying art in the galleries of Italian cities, he paid particular attention to the compositional skill of the Old Masters, an interest that would certainly be reflected later in his own photography.

After philosophy, the next stage of a Jesuit student's formation is called 'Regency', a period spent teaching boys at secondary school. Frank was assigned to Belvedere.

Back in Ireland, In 1909 a rather special summer holiday came Frank's way. His Uncle Robert, the Bishop of Cloyne, brought him to Rome by sea via Lisbon. The bishop's sister, Mary Browne, was serving in the papal household. She was able to make arrangements for uncle and nephew to have breakfast with His Holiness. Afterwards, Frank was able to photograph Pope (now Saint) Pius X.

Frank's studies continued at Milltown Park in south Dublin from 1911 to 1916, where he studied theology and philosophy. Jesuits study theology for four years, being ordained priests after the third of these. Frank Browne was ordained to the priesthood on 31 July, 1915.

On 3 April 1912, he received a letter that would change the course of his life. The letter came from the White Star Line and it contained a first-class ticket for the first two legs of the maiden voyage of the *Titanic*. The letter he received from the White Star Line wished Frank 'an enjoyable trip' aboard its newest liner, the largest ship afloat. His ticket for the voyage was addressed to him at the Bishop's House, Queenstown, because it was Uncle Robert who had paid his fare. As well as providing the ticket, Bishop Browne probably purchased the camera with which Frank was to record the famous voyage.

The morning of Wednesday 10 April found Frank on the platform of Waterloo Station in London, ready to board 'the first and last *Titanic Special*.' When the train pulled up alongside the dock in Southampton, Frank was astonished by the immensity of the liner. His first glimpse of the *Titanic* was from the first-class gangway, which led

1, Cockspur Street, S.W.
"Oceanic House."
Telegraphic Address: "Vessels, London."
38, Leadenhall Street, E.C.
London.
Telegraphic Address: "Ismay, London."
Canute Road, Southampton.
Telegraphic Address: "Ismay, Southampton."
9, Broadway, New York.
Telegraphic Address: "Ismay, New York."
84, State St., Boston.
Telegraphic Address: "Ismay, Boston."
118, Notre Dame St. West, Montreal.
Telegraphic Address: "Ismay, Montreal."
21, Piazza della Borsa, Naples.
Telegraphic Address: "Ismay, Naples."
Via Alla Nunziata, No. 18, Genoa.
Telegraphic Address: "Ismay Genoa."
Paris Agent: Nicholas Martin, 9, Rue Scribe.
Telegraphic Address: "Ismay, Paris."
30, James St., Liverpool.
Telegraphic Address: "Ismay, Liverpool."

White Star Line Services.

Southampton-Cherbourg-New York.
Royal & United States Mail Steamers.
Via Queenstown (Westbound)-Plymouth (Eastbound)

Liverpool-New York.
Via Queenstown.

Liverpool-New York.
(Freight.)

Liverpool-Boston.
Via Queenstown.

Liverpool-Quebec-Montreal.

Liverpool-Australia.
Via South Africa.

Liverpool-Australia.
(Freight.)

Liverpool-New Zealand.
(Freight.)

London-New Zealand.
Via South Africa.

New York-Mediterranean.
Via Azores.

Boston-Mediterranean.
Via Azores.

Through Bookings
to all parts
of the world.

WHITE STAR LINE.
JAMES SCOTT & Co. *Agents*.

Telegrams:- "ISMAY." Queenstown.
Telephone No. 3.

Passenger. *Department*.

Scott's Square,
QUEENSTOWN, April 3rd. 1912.

"OLYMPIC." (TRIPLE SCREW) 45.324 TONS
"TITANIC." (TRIPLE SCREW) 45.000 TONS
THE LARGEST STEAMERS IN THE WORLD

Dear Father Browne, "First Class"

We have pleasure in handing you herewith pass from Southampton to Queenstown per s.s. "Titanic" April 10th, and we trust you will have an enjoyable trip.

Yours truly,
FOR JAMES SCOTT & Co.,

The Rev. F.M. Browne. S.J.
Bishop's Palace,
Queenstown.

The letter from the White Star Line that included Fr Browne's first-class ticket for the first two legs – Southampton to Cherbourg, Cherbourg to Cobh – of the maiden voyage of the *Titanic*

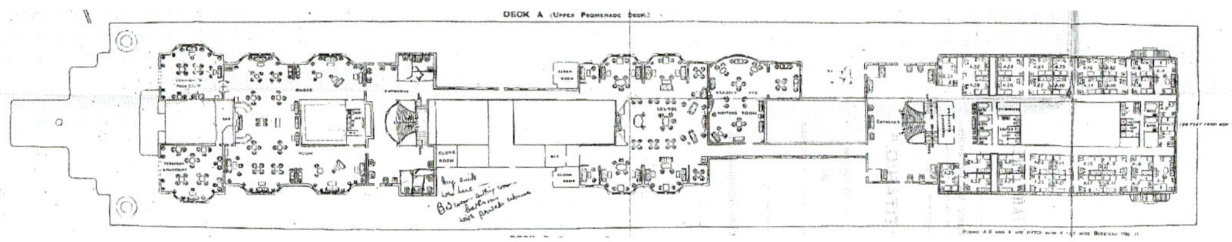

Fr Browne's cabin, A37, was at the top of the famous staircase, to the right. This room, and A36 opposite, were additions to the design for the sister ship, *Olympic*, and their exclusion is proof that the *Titanic* ship plan was, in fact, the *Olympic* ship plan. On this plan, Fr Browne has scribbled a drawing of both cabins

out of an upper storey of the station. He stopped to photograph the second-class gangway 'over one hundred and fifty yards away'. On stepping aboard the liner, he was handed a plan of the ship in order to help him locate his stateroom, number A37. This plan still exists among his other memorabilia of the voyage. There is a note in Frank's handwriting on the top, pointing out that although the plan is headed *Titanic* this is actually a plan of the sister ship, *Olympic*. Thomas Andrews, the Managing Director of Harland and Wolff who built the liner in Belfast, helped Frank to find his stateroom since he was looking for A36 for himself. A steward gave them the helpful advice that it was 'somewhere for'ard'.

After breakfast next morning there was plenty of time for more photographs of different parts of the liner, passengers of three classes and members of the crew, including Captain Edward Smith walking alone along the Promenade Deck. Frank was the only person ever to take a photograph of the ship's Marconi-room. It shows Mr Harold Bride at the controls, and the caption tells us that he was 'afterwards saved'.

Frank made numerous friends during his short voyage – Southampton to Cherbourg, Cherbourg to Cobh – and continued to correspond with survivors and

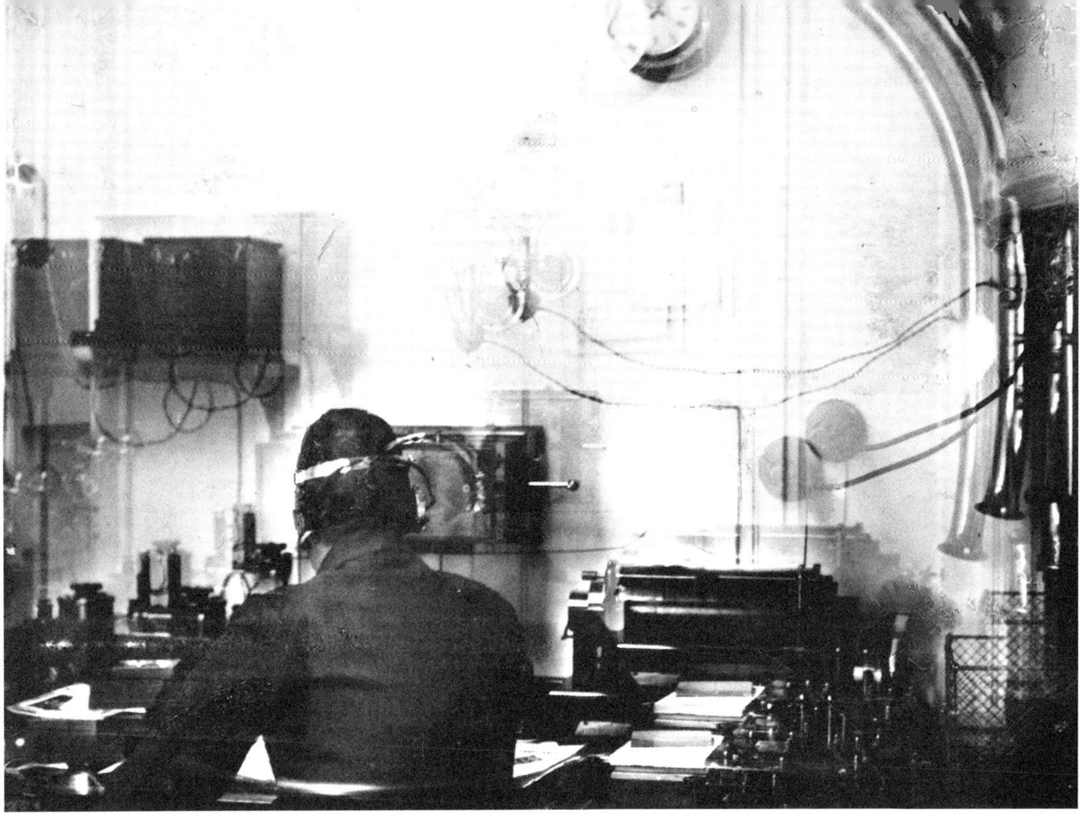

Fr Browne's own caption reads, 'In the Marconi Room: Mr Harold Bride, afterwards saved, sitting at the table. Two exposures on the one plate! This is the only photo ever taken of the Marconi Room of the *Titanic*'

with relatives of the deceased for years after the tragedy. An American family offered to pay his fare for the third leg of the *Titanic's* passage, out of Cobh to New York. From the Marconi-room, Harold Bride sent a message to the Provincial Superior of the Jesuits in Dublin asking if Frank could stay on board. By the time they reached Cork harbour, there was an answering message for Frank. It said, succinctly, 'GET OFF THAT SHIP. PROVINCIAL'.

In later years, Frank Browne used to say that it was the only time that Holy Obedience had saved a man's life! Anyhow, off that ship he had to get. And from the tender at Queenstown he took the last extant photograph of Captain Smith gazing, ironically, into a life-boat.

When news of the *Titanic* disaster reached Ireland, Frank was already back at his studies in Milltown Park, Dublin. Suddenly he became famous. His photographs of the maiden voyage were published on the front pages of newspapers across the world.

When, seventy-six years later in 1986, Robert Ballard found the wreck of the *Titanic* beneath the surface of the Atlantic, he was able to prove that the liner had split in two and that the bow section was lying 1,970 feet apart from the stern section of the

Left: Chaplains, Father Browne and Father Scannell at Arras, 1918. Above: Karsh portrait sent by Lord Alexander to Father Browne. Yousuf Karsh was a photographer known for his portraits of notable individuals. Lord Alexander described Fr Browne as, 'the bravest man I ever met'

ship. Uncannily the split cut right through staterooms A36 and A37: the former being that of the Managing Director of Harland and Wolff, the latter belonging for two days to Father Browne.

Early in 1916 an appeal for war chaplains reached the Provincial from the Chief Chaplain to the Forces, London. In order to oblige, the final examinations in Milltown Park were moved forward so that those volunteering for the army could depart as soon as possible. Before Easter (i.e. before the Easter Rising in Dublin), Father Browne had joined the First Battalion of the Irish Guards. He was to serve in the front line in France and Flanders right up to the end of the war in November 1918. Injured five times, he had to have his whole jaw wired up on one occasion, and he was gassed once. He won the Military Cross and Bar and the *Croix de Guerre.* He was also decorated by the King of the Belgians and was described by his commanding officer, Colonel (later Field-Marshall Earl) Alexander as 'the bravest man I ever met'.

In July 1920, Frank completed his Jesuit training, postponed during the war, and was assigned to teach in Belvedere College once more. He resumed the editorship of *The Belvederian* and took over the running of the Camera Club and the Cycling Club once more. During his first term in Belvedere, on 31 October, he cycled up to the Vice-regal Lodge in the Phoenix Park to make a personal appeal to Lord French on behalf of the Irish patriot, Kevin Barry. But to no avail: the Belvedere boy was executed in Mountjoy Jail next morning.

In 1922 he was appointed Superior of St Francis Xavier's Church, on Gardiner Street, Dublin. Although it was not a parish church at the time, it was a very busy place, running many specialised sodalities and providing a pulpit for the numerous famous preachers of those days. Dubliners flocked to Gardiner Street for the Novena of Grace, the Sacred Heart Devotions and for the lectures of Professors from Milltown Park. Father Browne carried out many practical improvements, such as the installation of a loudspeaker system and the replacement of antiquated central heating.

In the middle of all this activity, his health began to deteriorate. His lungs were increasingly giving him trouble. His doctor recommended dry air and a warmer climate, so early in 1924 he left to spend two years in Australia. Father Browne took dozens of pictures during the voyage out, mostly showing the passengers at play and the members of the crew at work. When the ship arrived at Melbourne, Father Browne felt very much at home because he was met by a group of Irish Jesuits, several of whom had joined the Order on the same day as himself.

In over a thousand pictures of Australia which he took before the end of 1925, we see that he was able to attend horse-races at Melbourne, yacht-races at Sydney, cricket test matches against England at Adelaide and Brisbane, as well as sheep-shearing competitions at Kangaroobie. Furthermore, he travelled for over three thousand miles in the outback.

The return journey to England began with a voyage on the *Orama* from Perth to

Street Scene, Port Said, Egypt, 1925

The West Front of York Minster, 1926

Ceylon, now Sri Lanka, via the Cocos Islands. From Ceylon he travelled via Somaliland and Yemen to Aiden. Then, past Ethiopia, Sudan and Saudi Arabia, his ship sailed on through the Red Sea to Suez. Passing through that canal, he photographed life in Egypt on both the African and Asian banks before arriving in Port Said. From Port Said he sailed across the Mediterranean Sea, first to Salonika in Greece and then, past Mount Etna on Sicily, to Naples. A three-day stopover there gave him the opportunity to visit Pompeii and photograph its extraordinary remains.

His next ship took him to Toulon in the south of France, then to Gibraltar where he took some fine pictures of the rock itself and then crossed into Spain to visit Algeciras and La Linea. From Gibraltar he voyaged to Lisbon and from the Portuguese capital it was non-stop to Plymouth with a rough passage through the Bay of Biscay.

After a short stay in England, Father Browne returned to his post at St Francis

Xavier church, Gardiner Street, once more in full health. He stayed in this post from the end of 1925 to the end of 1928. With his lungs cured, permanently as it turned out, his fame as a preacher increased: people would come from distant parts to hear his sermons.

It was also in 1925 that he began to photograph Dublin city extensively. In due course he would take nearly five thousand pictures of the capital, the final roll of film being shot in 1957. He took lessons as a pilot in 1926. His Dublin photographs include many of the city and suburbs taken from the air. For the most part, the quality of these was poor, as he was the first to admit, but there are several excellent views of the city and of the Malahide area in north County Dublin.

In the summer of 1926, Father Browne travelled to England where he had been asked to give a retreat to the nuns of the Bar Convent, York. He took dozens of photographs of that ancient city, its walls and gates, its shambles and its Minster. Before returning to Ireland, he visited the Jesuit boarding-school, Stonyhurst College, in Lancashire. He recalled that Conan Doyle had been a pupil there and had used Stonyhurst and its grounds as the setting for his masterpiece, *The Hound of the Baskervilles*. Of course, Hopkins was also a student, and later a teacher, at Stoneyhurst, so he walked in the footsteps of his companion in this book.

By 1927 Father Browne was a member of the Photographic Society of Ireland and of the Dublin Camera Club. He exhibited some of his own work and won numerous prizes.

All this time Father Browne's reputation as a preacher in Gardiner Street continued to grow: so much so, that his next assignment was to the Mission and Retreat Staff of the Irish Jesuits, a post he would occupy for the next thirty years. During 1929 he began a routine that he was to follow for many years, travelling continually from parish to parish, mainly by train. The work suited Father Browne admirably. He soon found that nearly all of his work was to be done in the evenings, which left him free for most of the day to pursue photography.

In the middle of 1930 the Jesuit move to Emo, Co Laois finally took place. Emo Court was designed by James Gandon for George Dawson, first Earl of Portarlington, in 1790. A curved corridor, named the Serpentine, led to a separate building to the left of the main house known (for some obscure reason dating back to the Portarlington days) as the 'Bachelors' Quarters'. It was in this block that Father Browne acquired the room that would be his haven and his photo-laboratory until 1957. Now that he had a permanent base, Father Browne was able to set up his photographic equipment more satisfactorily. He coaxed the electricians who were re-wiring the main house at Emo to do a major job on his room, giving him two batches of electric sockets, ample power-points for his growing number of accessories. He had special blinds and curtains fitted to his window so that it could be converted into a dark-room within seconds.

Early in 1932, knowing that it would be put to good use, his Uncle Robert gave him a present of a Kodak 16mm cine-camera. His first 16mm movie, entitled 'The Eucharistic congress of 1932' was exhibited in Dublin to great acclaim.

In subsequent years Father Browne made quite a few other 16mm motion-pictures. The best known of these was his history of the Foxford Woollen Mills in County Mayo. Most of the other films made by Father Browne were commissioned by a variety of governmental or educational bodies. For instance, he made a film on Forestry Work at Emo for the Department of Agriculture; a film on the Garda Siochana for the Commissioner of Police, General Eoin O'Duffy; a documentary on Irish Creameries for the Department of Industry and Commerce; a history of the rural electrification of Ireland for the Electricity Supply Board.

Between 1933 and the outbreak of Second World War in 1939 Father Browne's work as a missioner brought him to many parishes in England, Wales and Scotland. During the summer of 1933 Father Browne paid a visit to the Kodak Works at Harrow, near London, where he was able to photograph cameras being manufactured and where he had an important interview with the Managing Director, George Davison who arranged for him to receive a free supply of film for life. By way of return, Father Browne used to make regular contributions to *The Kodak Magazine*.

In England, Father Browne photographed most of the Church of England cathedrals and also took pictures of many of the Roman Catholic ones, some of which were

Father Browne's photolab at Emo, County Laois, 1931

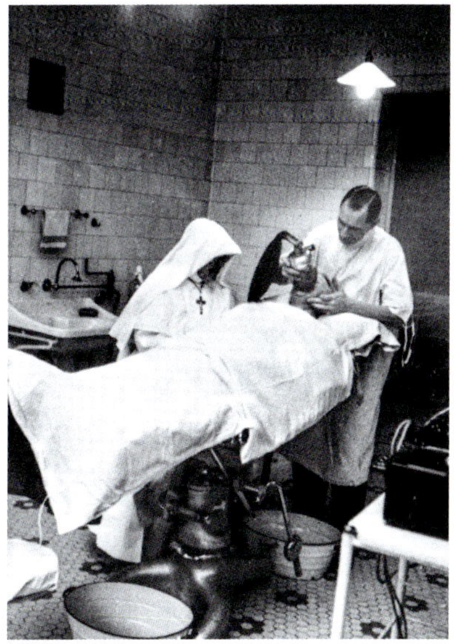

'Self under Anaesthetic', St Vincent's Hospital, Dublin, 1938

still in the course of construction. He visited London on many occasions and took remarkable photographs of the capital, including several on the Underground railway system. When staying overnight in London, often he availed of Lord Alexander's standing offer of accommodation. It was while he was in London that Father Browne visited the British Museum which commissioned him to photograph certain antiquities of England. He gave a lot of time to this important work and afterwards, when he had returned to Ireland, continued a lengthy correspondence with the Museum.

During 1937 and 1938 the Governing Body of the Church of England commissioned him to photograph the churches of East Anglia, inside and outside, concentrating on any unusual details. As a precaution against bomb damage, the Church of England wanted to ensure that its buildings could be restored with precision.

In 1938 Father Browne was diagnosed with appendicitis and was committed to the care of the Irish Sisters of Charity at St Vincent's hospital, at that time located on St Stephen's Green. Before his appendectomy, the photographer mounted his camera on a tripod in the operating-theatre and set it on time-hold so as to be able to caption a picture, 'Self under Anaesthetic'. An early example of the now commonplace 'selfie', and an unusual example of self-revelation at that time.

Father Browne continued his photographic work during the Emergency years of the second world war. Still working with nitrate film, he made many nature studies of 'Trees', 'Seasons', 'Clouds', 'Flowers' and 'Animals', with dozens of photographs under each of these headings. Most of these nature photographs were taken with the new camera, a Contax 'Number Two' which Father Browne had been given by his brother-in-law in 1937.

Also during the Emergency, Father Browne continued to experiment with colour photography. Presumably because of the expense involved in colour photography, and presumably because his standing allocation of film from Kodak did not include colour stock, he restricted his experiments to marketable subjects which could be turned into postcards, such as views of Croagh Patrick and of Achill Island.

During the early 1950s, Father Browne found time to become a more active member of the Irish Photographic Society. But this time he attended meetings more as a tutor than as a learner. By way of teaching how to use 'lamps' in lighting interior photographs of buildings, he had as examples films he made while touring Ireland of the Great Houses and their owners.

Travel and all forms of transport were subjects dear to Father Browne's heart including trains, aircraft and ships, all of which he photographed extensively. As regards road transport, the Browne Collection has pictures of everything from trams to donkey-tandems, from bicycles to articulated lorries, from horses-and-carts to traction engines.

In 1957, after being based in Emo for the best part of thirty years, Father Browne was transferred to Milltown Park in Dublin where he had been ordained a priest forty-two years earlier. During the last three years of his life, Father Browne contributed to many newspapers and magazines in Ireland and England. Most of the Dublin newspapers published his photographs, as did the *Cork Examiner.* Magazines that carried features by Father Browne include *Country Life, The Tatler and Sketch, The Irish Digest, The Capuchin Annual, The London Weekly Illustrated, The Far East* and *Ireland of the Welcomes*.

Father Browne making motion-picture at Walsingham, Norfolk, 1933

In the summer of 1960 Father Browne was told that he was dying. Faithful to the last, Lord Alexander travelled from England to visit him on his death-bed.

He died, much lamented, on 7 July 1960. His photos lay forgotten in the Jesuit Province Archives for the next 26 years, until they were re-discovered by Fr Eddie O'Donnell SJ who worked tirelessly for almost 30 years ensuring that the collection was both preserved and made known to the world.

In the Jesuit grave at Glasnevin Cemetery in Dublin lie the remains of Father Browne and of Gerard Manley Hopkins, among others.

Recommended Reading

Ballinger, Philip A., *The Poem as Sacrament: The Theological Aesthetic of Gerard Manley Hopkins*. Louvain: Peeters Press, 2000.

Davies, Walford, ed., with Introduction, *Gerard Manley Hopkins: the Major Poems*. London: Everyman's Library, 1979.

Desmond Egan, *Hopeful Hopkins: Essays*. Newbridge: Goldsmith Press, 2017.

Ellsberg, Margaret R., *Created To Praise*. Oxford: Oxford University Press, 1987.

Gardner, W. H., *Gerard Manley Hopkins: Poems, Prose Selected and Ed.* London: Penguin, 1972.

Lichtmann, Maria R., *The Contemplative Poetry of Gerard Manley Hopkins*. Princeton NJ: Princeton University Press, 1989.

– *Poetry as prayer: Gerard Manley Hopkins*. Boston MA: Pauline Press, 2002.

MacKenzie, Norman H., *A Reader's Guide to Gerard Manley Hopkins*. London: Thames & Hudson, 1981.

Mariani, Paul, *Gerard Manley Hopkins: A Life*. New York NY: Viking Press, 2008.

Mariani, Paul, *Commentary on the Complete Poems of Gerard Manley Hopkins*. London and Ithaca NY: Cornell University Press, 1970.

Martin, Robert B., *Gerard Manley Hopkins: A Very Private Life*. London: HarperCollins/Flamingo, 1992.

Nicholls, Aidan, OP, *Hopkins: Theologian's Poet*. Notre Dame IN: Ave Maria Press, 2006.

O'Donnell, E. E., *The Life and Lens of Father Browne*. Dublin: Messenger Publications, 2014

Phillips, Catherine, *Gerard Manley Hopkins: The Major Works*. Oxford: Oxford University Press, 2002.

Storey, Graham, *A Preface to Hopkins*. London: Longman Group, 1981.

White, Norman, *Hopkins: A Literary Biography*. Oxford: Clarendon Press, 2001.

(Endnotes)

1 Paul Mariani, *Gerard Manley Hopkins: A Life*. New York NY: Viking Press, 2008, 29–30, 33.

2 Catherine Phillips, *Gerard Manley Hopkins: The Major Works*. Oxford: Oxford University Press, 2002, 224–5.

3 Phillips, op. cit., 208.

4 Geoffrey Grigson, *Writers and Their Work, No, 59: Gerard Manley Hopkins*. Longmans, Green & Co., 1972, 8.

5 Phillips, op. cit., 304.

6 In Philip A. Ballinger, *The Poem as Sacrament: The Theological Aesthetic of Gerard Manley Hopkins*. Louvain: Peeters Press, 2000, 104.

7 Phillips, op. cit., 235.

8 Ballinger, op. cit., 43.

9 C. H. Plotkin, ed., *Soundings: Hopkins Studies in Transition*. Philadelphia: St Joseph University Press, 2007, 32.

10 Norman H. MacKenzie, *A Reader's Guide to Gerard Manley Hopkins*, London: Thames and Hudson, 1981, 238

11 Phillips, op. cit., 334.

12 Desmond Egan, *Hopeful Hopkins: Essays*. Newbridge: Goldsmith Press, 2017, *xiv*. Egan is Artistic Director of the annual Gerard Manley Hopkins International Festival which is based at Newbridge College, County Kildare.

13 Norman White, *Hopkins: A Literary Biography*. Oxford: Clarendon Press, 2001, 22.

14 Phillips, op. cit., 347.

15 Aidan Nicholls, *Hopkins: Theologians's Poet*. Notre Dame IN: Ave Maria Press, 2006, 33.

16 Phillips, op. cit., 304.

17 MacKenzie, op. cit., 88.

18 Ibid.

19 Ibid., 89.

20 Paul Mariani, *Commentary on the Complete Poems of GMH*. London and Ithaca NY: Cornell University Press, 1970, 141.

21 Ibid., 169–70.

22 From an article by Seamus Heaney in *Preoccupations: Selected Prose, 1968–1978*. London: Faber & Faber, 1980, 79–97.

23 Phillips, op.cit., 240.

24 Mariani, *Commentary on the Poems of Gerard Manley Hopkins*, op. cit.,177.

25 MacKenzie, op. cit., 146.

26 MacKenzie, op. cit., 151.

27 Mariani, *Commentary on the Poems of Gerard Manley Hopkins*, op. cit., 193.

28 Mariani, *Commentary on the Poems of Gerard Manley Hopkins*, op. cit., 196.

29 Robert B. Martin, *Gerard Manley Hopkins: A Very Private Life*. London: HarperCollins/Flamingo, 1992, 360.

30 Ibid., 362.

31 Phillips, op. cit., Lettter to Dixon, 252.

32 Mariani, *Gerard Manley Hopkins: A Life*, op. cit., *338*.

33 Mariani, ibid., 376.

34 Norman White, op. cit., 357.

35 Martin, op. cit., 386.

36 Mariani, *Commentary on the Complete Poems of Gerard Manley Hopkins*, op. cit., 220.

37 MacKenzie, op. cit., 184.

38 Martin, *Gerard Manley Hopkins: A Life*, op. cit., 379.

39 Mariani, *Commentary on the Complete Poems of Gerard Manley Hopkins*, op. cit., 231–2.

40 Mariani, *Gerard Manley Hopkins: A Life*, op. cit., 357.

41 MacKenzie, op. cit., 186.

42 Mariani, *Commentary on the Complete Poems of Gerard Manley Hopkins*, op. cit., 239–41.

43 Paul Mariani, *Commentary, 288,ft 37.*

44 MacKenzie, op. cit., 195.

45 Mariani, *Gerard Manley Hopkins: A Life*, op. cit., 403.

46 Phillips, op. cit., 264.

47 MacKenzie, op. cit., 204.

48 Mariani, *Commentary on the Complete Poems of Gerard Manley Hopkins*, op. cit., 303–4.

49 Ballinger, op. cit., 2.

50 Phillips, op. cit., 229.

51 Ibid., 219.

52 Nicholls, op. cit., 191.

53 Elizabeth Schneider, *The Dragon at the Gate: Studies in the Poetry of Gerard Manley Hopkins*. Oakland CA: University of California Press, 1968, 261f.

Dr Jo O'Donovan is a Sister of Mercy who taught in the areas of RE and Theology and Religious Studies in Mary Immaculate College, Limerick. Having developed inter-faith dialogue with theology students, she published, on retirement, *Understanding Differently: Christianity and the World Religions* (Dublin: Veritas, 2012). Always a lover of poetry, she now works with a group of poetry readers and gives occasional workshops. Hopkins has been special for her. Having been to St Beuno's in Wales, and having walked his roads and climbed his hills, she says Hopkins is all essence. He teaches us what poetry is. This book has been written with an eye to poetry lovers' needs, whether for private reading or in a group. The commentaries are offered as stimulants and clarifications to be finally put aside when one reads the poems for oneself. As a wording of Divine Beauty, Hopkins' poetry is also a theology.